Praise for *Last to Eat, Last to Learn*

"Pashtana's story highlights the resourcefulness and bravery of young women in Afghanistan. I hope readers will be inspired by her mission to give every girl the education she deserves and the opportunity to pursue her dreams." —Malala Yousafzai

"Pashtana's voice is once-in-a-generation. A born leader who took her own dreams and broke them into a thousand pieces to share with others. Her story is an inspiration. Her work, a mission—more necessary now than ever. Pashtana Durrani came to live out loud. And we should all be listening." —Amna Nawaz, co-anchor PBS NewsHour

"Who should read Pashtana Duranni's *Last to Eat, Last to Learn*? Anyone who believes that inspired, imaginative, and sometimes irrational ideas can change lives. Anyone who refuses to accept 'it's impossible' as a reason not to pursue her passion. Anyone who doubts that determined, driven leadership can overcome even obstacles like Taliban bombs. And anyone who still thinks it's a good idea to impose Western values and ways of doing things on the peoples of the Global South. Pashtana Duranni's journey is uplifting and optimistic because she constantly gets up after being knocked down by the cruel realities of life in Pakistan and her native Afghanistan. Her story is testimony to how one determined leader, with irrational passion and a deep commitment to educating young girls, can make a lasting difference." —Alan Stoga, Chairman, Tällberg Foundation

"As an American, I meet many who know little and feel no likeness to the land where so many of our sons and daughters gave their lives. Idealistic yet logical, Pashtana serves as a portal between two seemingly divergent worlds, illuminating the shared human values that connect us. The relevance of her story has no bounds. It belongs in the hands of the politician as much as the soldier, the parent, or the child. While we may characterize Pashtana as an activist, or educator, let us first characterize her as a leader." —Major Jessica Yahn, Cultural Support Team, U.S. Army Special Operations Command

"Much praise to Pashtana Durrani for telling the world the riveting story of her work in the fight for girls' education in Afghanistan—a story of determination, triumph, and loss in the battle for girls and women's rights. As a young leader and activist for girls' education, she is an exceptional role model for girls around the world, exemplifying the power of determination and passion in achieving the nearly impossible."

—Mursel Sabir, Founder, Afghans Empowered

"This book is the breathtaking story of a young activist who will make history. The courage and intelligence of this one-of-a-kind young woman shine through in every line and take us to the heart of the fight for girls' education in Afghanistan. This first-hand account allows us to discover the Pashtun people through the eyes of a girl who is both independent-minded and respectful of traditions. Pashtana Durrani shares an acute and clever insight into the origins of the Taliban, a moving childhood story in an Afghan refugee camp in Pakistan, and an incredible journey against the odds to empower girls. Pashtana Durrani has a unique and fascinating destiny. She's been both discriminated against and privileged, she understands Afghanistan and Pashtun society as well as Western culture. She brings an enlightened view of these two worlds that do not understand each other. As Pashtana Durrani is taking every risk to empower and educate Afghan girls, she is living proof that Afghan girls are strong and intelligent and deserve our solidarity."

—Marina Wutholen, Director of dev.tv and Founder
Young Activists Summit

"Pashtana's story is not only one of gender empowerment, it is one of communal pragmatism and realization that together, men and women in Afghanistan, for the sake of their community, can transcend barriers and transform their society for long-term prosperity and peace."

—Dr. Victoria C. Fontan, Professor of Peace and Conflict
Studies and Vice President of Academic Affairs at the
American University of Afghanistan

"With a spirit that echoes through these pages and a voice that rises above the din, Pashtana Durrani shares her compelling story and mission to empower women in Afghanistan. Having worked with Pashtana, I am in awe of her consistent drive towards bringing innovative learning solutions to women and girls in Afghanistan, despite socio-political instability in the country. This book is a reflection of her spirit—bright, passionate, driven."

—Tanya Qadir, Director of Partner Success, Rumie Initiative

Last to Eat, Last to Learn

LAST TO EAT, LAST TO LEARN

My Life in Afghanistan
Fighting to Educate Women

PASHTANA DURRANI
AND TAMARA BRALO

CITADEL PRESS
Kensington Publishing Corp.
www.kensingtonbooks.com

CITADEL PRESS BOOKS are published by

Kensington Publishing Corp.
119 West 40th Street
New York, NY 10018
Copyright © 2024 Pashtana Dorani and Tamara Sabljak Bralo

All Kensington titles, imprints, and distributed lines are available at special quantity discounts for bulk purchases for sales promotions, premiums, fund-raising, educational, or institutional use. Special book excerpts or customized printings can also be created to fit specific needs. For details, write or phone the office of the Kensington sales manager: Kensington Publishing Corp., 119 West 40th Street, New York, NY 10018, attn: Sales Department; phone 1-800-221-2647.

All photos courtesy of the author.

CITADEL PRESS and the Citadel logo are Reg. U.S. Pat. & TM Off.

ISBN: 978-0-8065-4244-7

First Citadel hardcover printing: March 2024

10 9 8 7 6 5 4 3 2 1

Printed in the United States of America

Library of Congress Control Number: 2023930892

ISBN: 978-0-8065-4246-1 (e-book)

To my father and the young girls of Afghanistan.

Last to Eat, Last to Learn

PROLOGUE

 SPENT THE ENTIRE YEAR OF 2016 DODGING SLIP-
pers my mother threw at me. It's a favorite
educational aid of displeased Pashtun mothers:
slippers fly in your direction most of your childhood, especially if, like me, you're less than obe-
dient and opiniated to no end. There's even a
term for it: a flying chaplak.

She's been trying to hit me with one ever
since I announced my decision not to go to Oxford. From the moment I uttered those words,
I didn't even have to open my mouth for my
mother to reach for her slipper. Seeing me sufficed.

I grew up in a refugee camp in Pakistan, one
of four million Afghans living there at the time,

displaced by decades of war. Everything in my life was geared toward education. It was the only way to leave the refugee life behind. The odds were near impossible, but I made it. I was admitted into a yearlong preparatory program in Oxford. An essay I wrote led to an offer of a full scholarship. It wasn't an admittance to the university itself, it was merely a geographical coincidence, but it felt like a sign. We had it all planned: I was going to ace that preparatory program, then I was going to get myself admitted to Oxford University proper and study philosophy, politics, and economics. Oxford was my dream. Women I admired came from around the world to study at Oxford and became amazing leaders. Oxford wasn't just a school; it was a mythical place that turned young girls into heroines. I was going to be one of them.

Until I wasn't.

It wasn't a sudden decision. There was always a nagging thought in the back of my mind that I didn't have time for all that. My reluctance wasn't about fear: I was eighteen, I thought I could do anything. I didn't know enough about the world to be scared. I'd never been to England, and the only place there that I'd heard of was Oxford. Not even London. What I wanted, what I dreamed of, were rows and rows of leather-bound books and my own education.

Yet I had suspected for a while that what I *needed* to do was something else entirely: I needed to continue to fight for the education of other girls like me.

Educating girls was our family business.

My father opened a school for our community with his own money decades ago. The school didn't require much: he blocked off two rooms in our house and put family members to work. My aunt taught there. My mother taught there. I started teaching English there at the age of seven; I'd come back from my private lessons and teach the girls everything I learned in class.

It didn't take much introspection to see that I was different. We, too, were refugees, but my family's life differed greatly from those around us. My father was a tribal leader, like his father before him, and his grandfather before him. Once established, hierarchy and privilege travel with you—even to a refugee camp. Although most of the ancestral land the family owned was made inaccessible by war, we were lucky enough to have a well-established business on the Pakistani side, too. He could afford to educate me the way the Pakistani middle class educated their girls—with tutors and obligatory English classes.

My father loved history. Kids obsess over Disney princesses all over the world, but my father didn't approve of them. Growing up, he kept drumming into me: "You don't need fairy tales, Pashtana, you need history. There are so many Afghan women who mattered far more than those princesses." Truthfully, it was difficult to see the difference between the two. At that time, Afghanistan was under the Taliban rule, and Cinderella looked only slightly less fictional than the Afghan heroines of the past. But I understood what he was saying: no one is coming to save you if you're an Afghan woman.

My entire childhood, my father insisted that I should be of service to my community. He's the one who kept teaching me history. He's the one who insisted that I mattered too, despite being a girl. He's the one who kept telling me to keep my eyes open to the troubled world around me. "Don't take your education for granted. Just look around! Education is a privilege. It shouldn't be, but it is."

I listened. I did what he asked me to do, I looked around. I saw the camp that had no running water, no electricity. Girls around me were going hungry and illiterate; most of them have never left the camp. Once they marry, they don't even leave their homes. For too many of them, death is the only opportunity for mobility.

In most Afghan households, girls can only eat after all the men are done eating. The father eats first, then the sons, then, if there's anything left, it's a girl's turn. Often, in the poorest of the families, there's nothing left. Education is no different. Girls are meant to wait their turn until we're done educating boys. Not that anyone is trying hard to educate boys, either: with Afghanistan perpetually at war, there's little learning to be had before they get to pick up guns. We always seem to wait for something. We wait for the fighting to stop, for schools to open, generation after generation. When it comes to education, Afghans are the most patient people in the world.

I, too, was waiting. I spent years learning about Afghanistan, but I had never seen the land. It was too broken, never safe enough to visit, let alone move back to. I wanted to help bring about change, but Oxford would add at least four more years to that perpetual holding pattern. If the point of my going to Oxford was to eventually help Afghan girls, how many of them could afford to wait for me? How many would I lose during those four years it would take to finish?

I was an accidental activist. In the beginning, I was just trying to stand up for myself. I was relentlessly bullied growing up: by my cousins for being a girl, by my schoolmates for having tribal roots, and by the state system for being a refugee. My refusal to tolerate it had far wider-reaching consequences on my life than I had originally intended. If you're a tribal woman, the bar for activism is low. Trained our entire lives to be neither seen nor heard, whenever one of us tries to raise her voice, it becomes a political act.

Shutting up never seemed like an option, though. I was born loud, and whatever the consequences of speaking up might have been, suffering in silence seemed so much worse. At first I just tormented my family with my views on educating women, a cause I made my own. I quickly branched out to sharing them with my friends. By the time I was sixteen, an Afghan paper published my first op-ed on the rights of refugee girls. It was hardly controversial, but in a country where dissenting voices are faithfully policed, it's not difficult to get noticed. There weren't many of us speaking up.

To leave for Oxford now seemed selfish, it seemed like a betrayal of everything I stood for. I was already privileged. I already had a head start other girls could only dream of.

I don't think I deserved those flying chaplaks at all. Not going to Oxford was my father's fault, really. He started it.

Oxford was the fairy tale.

I chose history, so I packed my bags and went to Afghanistan instead.

1

THE STREET I GREW UP ON WAS THE LAST FRON-
tier of a city, just before the refugee camp
started in earnest, an invisible border between
those who belonged and those who didn't. It was
where the paved roads stopped. Once you got
inside the camp, there was only a labyrinth of
dirt paths. The deeper you went in, the smaller
the buildings, until they disappeared altogether
and you reached the area where there was nothing but tents.

New people kept coming to Pakistan almost
daily, and the old ones never left. War in Afghanistan started some forty years ago, and there were
millions of Afghans that never saw Afghanistan. I
was one of them. I was a third-generation refugee.

It was my grandmother, Khan Bibi, who brought the family here, having fled the war and her marriage in one fell swoop. Tales about Khan Bibi—so far from our reality, from our life—felt like fairy tales. It was only the softening in my father's voice whenever he spoke of her that brought her to life as a real person.

Khan Bibi was educated, by the standards of her time anyway, and able to recite most of the Quran by heart. She grew up in a castle. The drawbridge that connected the castle to the village would be raised every night and lowered in the morning, and the noise of the chain was so loud it would wake up the people of Maruf. She had women to help her get dressed and braid her hair. She didn't want for anything.

My mother would tell me how later in life, every now and then, random details from the opulent sets of Indian soap operas would reduce Khan Bibi to tears: she'd be reminded of the drapes, or the window from the house in which she grew up. She moved away after she got married, but that castle was the house she always remembered as home.

My grandparents lived a happy life, by all accounts. That is, until after some minor argument, my grandfather decided to take a second wife. That's when all hell broke loose. My grandmother would have none of it. Islam may allow for more than one wife, but it wasn't practiced often among the upper classes. It was an insult.

Don't do it, she warned him.

Don't do it, the sons warned him.

By the early 1980s, war was already all around them. My grandfather was a mujahedeen commander in the fight against the Soviets. As far as he was concerned, he was the one issuing orders, not the one taking them. With a stubbornness that is hereditary, he decided to spite them all and go ahead and marry his second wife.

But Khan Bibi wasn't the kind to back down, either. The night her husband got married, in a deliberately lavish ceremony designed to drive the wedge deeper, Khan Bibi sat all of her children down and gave them the option of leaving with her or staying with their father.

All eleven of them decided to go with her.

Khan Bibi didn't have time to pack. They left that same night without taking with them even a change of clothes. She headed to her parents' house, but their village was already a battlefield. Unable to stay there, she fled to Pakistan. Somewhere along the way, she acquired a cow from her family, to feed the brood.

The woman who grew up having everything, who grew up having everything done for her, was now scrubbing other people's houses to survive. Instead of making her children earn wages, as most Afghans in that situation would, she sent all of them to school, girls and boys. It was up to her—and the cow—to ensure their survival. The kids went barefoot for years, but all of them finished college, and most of them have advanced degrees.

It wasn't long before my grandfather had to flee too—and came to settle in the same camp. My father, always a peacemaker, reconciled his parents, and he and his brothers were allowed back in my grandfather's life. Being recognized again as part of my grandfather's lineage restored their claim to tribal leadership. But privilege came late in life, too late for him to ever forget the struggle it took to get there. It was Khan Bibi to whom they owed everything. It was she who forged our family path. She was the one to educate them all on a housecleaner's salary. It was Khan Bibi's voice, determined and suffering no fools, that echoed through everything we were taught about women, about education, about poverty. She was the first to show us that a choice between food and education is not a choice at all. It became a guiding light for my father, a torch I would continue to carry. Above all, to us, Khan Bibi was a symbol of the Afghanistan we lost.

By the time I was born, privilege was redefined. Our house

was the biggest in the camp, surrounded by cypress trees as if presiding over the camp. Our lawn was trimmed, the weeds pulled out. Unlike most families around us, we never went hungry. For Eid, kids would line up to get sweets. We were the only ones handing them out: we were the only ones who could afford it.

You notice them early, these little differences, these little advantages, sometimes in the silliest of things. In the camp, where very few people had any furniture, we were the only family that had a sofa. Every time someone in our community decided to throw a wedding, they would come to our house and borrow it for the reception. It wasn't a wedding unless the men were sitting on our sofa. That piece of furniture was better traveled than any of us.

I knew from a young age that my family was somehow different. My father was a *khan*, a tribal leader. Khans are in charge of all tribal affairs, from judging village disputes to dealing with other tribes. In my father's case, because we were refugees, he would also have to deal with Pakistani authorities and humanitarian aid agencies. People listened to him.

We are Pashtuns, members of a tribe that lives on both sides of the border between Afghanistan and Pakistan. The outside world calls the border the Durand Line, named after a man who randomly scribbled it across a map. It divides our Pashtun tribe in two, although we still move back and forth relatively unimpeded. Unlike India or Pakistan, Afghanistan was never successfully colonized, although many tried. There's an independent, stubborn streak to us.

Pakistan didn't look kindly on Pashtuns, especially the Afghan ones, the ones from the wrong side of the tracks. Suspicions of political involvement were enough for villagers to be taken in by the authorities for questioning, disappearing for weeks and months at a time. My father, whose casual-at-best respect for the Afghan-Pakistan border already made him unpopular with the

Pakistani authorities, would go and make inquiries about their whereabouts. Depending on the reasons for the villager's disappearance or sometimes, just the mood of the official in charge, my father would frequently end up detained and thrown in prison himself. The job of a tribal leader wasn't all perks and privilege.

My family distributed more than just sofas for weddings and sweets for Eid. When humanitarian aid arrived, my father would let everyone in the camp know. I remember so vividly my mother and aunt creating little packages and then handing them out: children first, then women. Men would go last. It's not the usual order of things in our part of the world, but it was our house and our rules.

Aid packages were off-limits to my family. I never really cared or questioned that rule until one day a shipment arrived with something I wanted badly: a purple geometry set containing a ruler, protractor, and compass. I was six years old and had absolutely no use for a geometry set, but they were so pretty, the shade of purple unlike anything I've seen before. I obviously needed one.

I begged and begged my father. I was normally able to wear him down easily, but this time around he flat-out refused. That was new. He never said no; I could get away with almost anything.

He said that the sets were meant for the older girls who needed them for school. "They can't afford to buy a geometry set. If you absolutely have to have a geometry set, I'll buy you one."

My father was usually very smart, but he clearly wasn't understanding either me or the gravity of the situation. There was nothing like those geometry sets here in Pakistan. He couldn't just buy one. I didn't need a geometry set. I needed the purple geometry set from the aid shipment.

He wouldn't budge. "You cannot take from your community if you're a good leader." It's a sound rule, I agreed, but surely there are always exceptions. Like the shiny purple geometry sets.

I lost the argument, not for the want of trying. It stayed with me though, this strict sense of fairness and justice he kept drumming into me—although it took growing up to understand it fully. To my father, leadership meant serving your people, putting them first, and he was grooming me, for as long as I can remember, to do the same.

I was the first of three children, two girls and a boy. The three of us couldn't have been more different in the way we looked or the way we behaved. I take after my father: I have dark hair; I am big and heavyset. My sister takes after my mother: lighter hair, lighter skin, and dainty. I was surly and forever arguing; she was outgoing and agreeable. Without my brother, you never would have guessed we were sisters. It was only looking at him, who got a bit from both parents, that would provide the connection. He, the youngest one, was the missing link.

Being a firstborn means nothing in Afghan society if you're a girl, but that too was different in our family. My father doted on me, treating me with the affection and attention normally reserved for sons. I'd trail him everywhere. He once left three hundred men waiting in order to finish drinking make-believe tea at a party with my dolls. I, of course, adored him right back. People seemed genuinely puzzled by his devotion to a daughter who, as it was pointed out in all seriousness, "wasn't even that pretty," the only criterion to judge a woman of any age. He didn't seem to care.

My father was among the first to go and fight against the Taliban after 9/11: I was four at the time. For me, the memory of the beginning of the war overlaps with the memory of the birth of my brother. The birth of a boy is a big deal in our culture, and my father was late to join the club: he got a son after eight years of marriage and two daughters. The celebrations spanned weeks.

People came from all over to visit and congratulate our family. Tribal leaders from across the region traveled to attend. I'd sit with my dad, at his feet, the only female of any age for as far as the eye could see, surrounded by all these men with turbans.

As time went by, the noise of celebrations quieted down, replaced by the hushed tones of conspiracies and war plans. The turbaned men that gathered now were leaders from all around Afghanistan, forming a tribal coalition against the Taliban.

From November or so, they would meet every day, until one evening I heard my father telling my mom: "We're moving tonight. We're going to go and take Kandahar." And then he was gone.

I didn't understand much of the world around me back then. I had no concept of the war, I didn't know what the Taliban was, or why my father would need to fight them. I didn't know they too were Pashtuns, like us. All I remembered of 9/11 was the entire village packed in one room watching grainy pictures of smoke and planes on the television. Ours was the only TV in the village, so everybody came to see what was going on. I can still see it clearly: men sitting around my brother's cradle; my sister all dolled up, wearing a beautiful red dress, probably thinking that all those people were there to see her. I can see myself clearly too: I was running around in a dress that was white in the morning when they put it on me, but later in the day didn't commit to any particular color.

I remember the feeling, not the event: the air was heavy, and with every collective, deep, shocked inhale it felt like there was less of it left to breathe. They would play it over and over, those planes crashing. It would be years before I was able to make the connection between those images and my father going to war.

When my father left, there were no phone calls, no information for weeks. My mother would sit and listen to the radio, a litany of villages and towns being fought over, won, and lost. That's how we found out that there was an attack on Spin Boldak, the town where my father was. After reporting about the fighting, after they'd gone through all the updates, the announcer would read the list of those killed.

My father's name was on it.

Everybody cried for days—everybody except for my mother. She sat there, motionless, speechless. To me, it seemed like she was the one who died.

No one in the family said anything to me; I was too young to understand. There was no help from my siblings: my brother was a baby, and my sister was two, so it was not as if I could have gone to them for an explanation. I just overheard grown-up conversations I didn't understand and noticed changes I couldn't explain. There were men coming back and forth through the women's quarters, where they're normally never allowed. It's a woman's private sanctuary, free of the outside regulations; you don't cover there, you dress differently. Normally, men were received outside in the guesthouse, not inside, and definitely not in women's quarters. For days, however, all sorts of strange people, men and women, walked around at all hours. They gathered around the phone in my mother's room, all waiting for something.

A week passed. I was in the garden to escape the gloom that permeated the house, digging as usual, when my father walked into the courtyard.

He was covered with dried blood. His head, hands, hips— it seemed like every part of his body was bandaged up. I think that was the first time I understood what war was: wounds and blood and waiting for people who may or may not come back. But despite the blood, despite those bandages, I could see it was him. The sight of blood didn't scare me. I ran toward him down the pathway. I remember falling in excitement, scraping my knee quite badly, but I picked myself up immediately and continued to run toward him. When I finally reached him, I held on to his leg screaming, "You're back, you're back!"

Suddenly, everybody was running out of the house. My mom came running toward him and hugged him. I remember that hug so clearly. Even I found it shocking: you really don't do that in our culture; you don't hug in public. We Pashtuns don't stand for a public display of emotions, and if you absolutely have to display emotions, you're best to restrict them to stubbornness, anger, and courage. My mother didn't seem to care. There she was, hugging my father. That's when she cried for the first time. It made no sense to me. It was over. Why cry now? My father was back from the dead.

When we finally allowed him to get into the house, to sit down, he told us how they came under attack from the Taliban. The building that housed his office was full of ammunition, and when a mortar hit it, it all just went up in the air. He had just stepped outside to clear his head. He kept saying how lucky he was, that he missed death by a few seconds. In that radio report, they listed everybody who was inside as dead, there was no point in checking after an explosion that big. He was the only survivor.

He stayed with us a week, to heal and recover before going back to fight. That would be the longest he stayed with us for a while. He wasn't well enough to go out, and I had him all to myself. Sure, my siblings and my cousins were there too, but I was sitting closest to him, and they all knew better than to try to come between us. As I sat at his feet, delighted by his unexpected presence, he told stories of Afghan heroines of the past. He talked about Malalai, about Queen Soraya. "Those women changed Afghanistan, and you can too. You just need to go to school and study," he said, looking at me.

I found the entire conversation confusing. I did go to school.

I didn't probe further, though; I was happy to have him back and, given the extent of his injuries, it didn't really seem like a good time to question him. I didn't know that the Taliban didn't allow women to leave the house, to work. I didn't know it had been a while since an Afghan woman succeeded at anything. I realize now those conversations were meant as a spoken will, that this brush with death made him see that the times were too uncertain to wait for me to grow up to hear what he wanted me to know.

After a while, when that initial push against the Taliban was over, he'd go off to war the way suburban men go to work in American movies. He'd go for a week to fight, leaving on Saturdays, early morning, before any one of us got up. When he'd come back, he'd bring us presents, as if he was returning from a business trip, not war. It was always books, invariably large leather-bound history tomes. Then he'd ask me to choose which one of them we'd read. The books were heavy and took all my strength to pick up, but I would carry one to him, sit on his lap, and listen to him read the passages about Kandahar, about our tribe, our family. I didn't understand everything he was saying, but it didn't matter. My love of reading goes back to those afternoons spent listening to my father's voice.

The official end of the war meant little to us in the camp. The Taliban was forced out of Kabul, but the area we were from continued to be a battlefield. In Afghanistan, winning means little and it's always temporary. There's no peace there, just a quick pause to reload the guns.

Strangely, I never worried about my father not coming back; I was always certain in my belief that he would return—even after that first scare. Maybe it's because he had such a presence. Even now that he really is gone, I still sometimes look up at the door thinking he's about to walk through it. I still expect him to defy the odds, one more time.

My mother came from an educated, although not exactly wealthy, family. She's a Pashtun too, she grew up in the urban area. My father saw her leaving school one afternoon and promptly fell in love. She was fourteen. He asked for her hand in marriage, but my mother's family wouldn't even consider giving their consent. Her family was integrated into Southern Pashtunkhuwa society, and wealthy or not, my father was a refugee. Naively, they thought that a simple rejection would put an end to the romance, but my father kept coming back for two years. An impasse required a change of tactic on his part: "I'm not asking anymore. I will marry her. She is the love of my life. I fell in love with her the moment I saw her." And with that they relented.

They got engaged and were married that same year. My mother was sixteen at the time. Two years later, I was born.

It was a love marriage, but that's apparently hardly a guarantee that things would go smoothly. Adjustments weren't easy for my mother. When we were alone as a family, she could be herself, but as soon as there were people around, it seemed like she had to be told every few minutes to cover up, or to listen better, or to understand more and talk less. Life wasn't easy on her, nor was the tribal structure she married into.

It wasn't just because she was a woman. Our gender dynamics are far more complicated than that. It's blood, too. As a daughter you can be empowered because you're born into a clan. But as a wife, if you marry out of your power base, you lose that privilege. I could follow my father into tribal meetings. I was even allowed to speak. My mother rarely left the house. I found it strange that even at the age of ten or so, my words carried more power than my mother's. I could cough, and my father would rush back from Afghanistan to take me to see a doctor. But when my mother fell ill, he was nowhere to be found for forty days. My uncles could boss her around with abandon, but as long as my father was around, they could never speak that way to me. I was blood, and she wasn't.

My upbringing was hardly traditional. For one, I was allowed to be a child, which is not a given in this part of the world. You're meant to work from the moment you could be useful. Not just chores, not just helping, you're meant to pull your weight in providing for the family. The streets of Kabul are full of five-year-olds who are the sole breadwinners in their family, selling knickknacks to passing cars.

My childhood was different. I had chores, but more often than not, I was running around with my cousins or digging in the garden. That kind of freedom was generally reserved for boys. Girls were meant to stay home, surrounded by grown-ups, never raising their voice, never expressing an opinion. It was training for marriage, for the rest of their lives. It was a way to teach the girls to accept without questioning, whatever horrible treatment came their way.

Whenever I describe my childhood to others, I always say that my parents were raising me as a tomboy, but that's not entirely accurate. Being a tomboy implies a choice to play with boys instead of girls, and I didn't make that choice. It's just that the boys were the only ones playing. In the camp, other than my sister and me, no other girls played at all.

Hanging out with boys gave me a different structure, a different understanding of the world. The only way for me to be heard in a group of my male cousins was to be louder and smarter. They were older than me, but still, being a daughter of a khan was as close to equality as an Afghan girl gets. I was able to find my place, or at least to fight for it.

It worked for a while, but once they turned ten or eleven, it seemed like it suddenly dawned on them that I was a girl. The boys discovered guns; they would trot around with ancient Kalashnikovs over their shoulders, suddenly important, suddenly grown-up, suddenly . . . manly. I had no patience for it. I still tried to boss them around. One of my cousins went to great lengths to explain to me that he, not I, should be a leader, because I was a woman and wouldn't amount to much anyway.

I am positive he didn't mean for me to interpret his comment as fighting words, but that's what they became. I started competing with that mouthy cousin of mine.

When I was ten, he got a new bike, an unimaginable luxury for a child. There were old bikes everywhere, used as a means of transportation for those lucky enough to get work, but a child having one—a new one, no less—was unheard of. I had to harass my father for a full week before he finally relented and got bikes for us too. My sister got a pretty pink one, with glitter. I got the blue one that looked just like my cousin's. But better. It was newer, shinier, and had fewer dents. Better.

My father knew me well.

I drove that bike around the backyard with steely determination, scandalizing everyone in sight. The older you get, the stricter the rules, and at ten, a girl is meant to cover up and shut up and finally retreat into the house. Not me. I'd show them who would amount to nothing.

2

CONTRARY TO THE POPULAR BELIEF, WE AFGHANS didn't discover education after 9/11 when aid organizations rolled into town. Before the Soviet invasion in 1979, most kids were in schools, but decades of war ground to a halt any efforts to continue with education. Forty years is a long time to stand still; people are just not wired for it. You are compelled to move after a while. So we started moving backward.

Our world started shrinking with the loss of land, but no one had it worse than women. Before, even in villages, it used to be normal for women to go outside, work in the fields, but by the time we reached refugee camps, women's movements were so restricted, we were left with no more than the kitchen and the backyard.

It all started innocently enough, as men trying to protect the women in their household. Restrictions had an air of common sense about them. It simply wasn't safe to go out. Camps were lawless stretches of no-man's-land, and refugees were vulnerable to everything: rape, abduction, acid thrown into girls' faces, and murder. As a result, women were locked up for their own good, as the story goes. Education was forgotten. Soon we forgot how we used to live; we didn't remember that we ever had it any different. We started believing this is how it always was.

That's where the Taliban came from. They were the boys running down dirt paths of Pakistani refugee camps, never encountering a woman they weren't related to. Once in power, that was the world they sought to reproduce.

Few in the refugee camp had access to Pakistani schools, and even then, girls would rarely be sent. My father, always the one to try to bring the mountain to Mohammed, tried to change that. He started a community school for girls in the 1990s, despite being a tribesman, despite people's resistance, and well before the West made it a popular cause.

He tried for years to get funding for the school from the aid agencies, but they insisted on a government-approved curriculum, which was impossible, not least because there was no government. Most aid agencies start their thinking from an ordered world of their own, not the chaotic one that we lived in. They required rules, commitments on all sides, or, at the very least, a community that wants it. They needed reassurances that were impossible to give.

My father instead favored a stealth approach, the educational equivalent of night banditry: reach as many girls as you can, teach as much you can, and try to outrun whatever is coming to crush them. Understandably, I suppose, that was not seen as a business plan.

Getting nowhere, my father finally decided to fund the school with his own money. He painted two classrooms light green ("For better learning," he'd explain to anyone who'd listen) and got it all going. All the women in my family taught there. At age seven, my job was to come back from my private English lessons and immediately teach the girls whatever I learned. There are still girls out there who can count to ten in English because of me.

While we were all involved, it was my aunt that ruled the school from the very beginning. My father's word as a khan carried a lot of weight, but the school was new, and the idea went against everything that the community had settled into. It was bound to take some persuading. Enter my aunt. She was more than happy to deal with any initial reluctance of the villagers.

In my aunt's retelling, there's a definitive Pashtun spin on ensuring school attendance; if a girl didn't show up at school, my aunt would show up at her house to try to reason with her family.

When that failed, as it inevitably did, she threatened to send one of my uncles to beat up whichever family member had the misfortune of opening the door to her. She meant it, too, pointing to one of her brothers who was lurking in the shadows, probably not entirely sure what he was doing there. We all did what she told us to; there were no follow-up questions with my aunt. Needless to say, thanks to her interventions, the school attendance improved dramatically.

With the attendance issues now sorted, my father set up a council of female elders to promote the school in a slightly less menacing manner than the bullying practiced by my aunt. It was a girl's school, run by women and housed in the women's quarters of our house.

It would have been difficult to grow up in a family like that and not get obsessed about education, and being a girl was always an added incentive. My mother was fond of saying, "If you want to make a name in this community, you have to study. That's how women get respect. If you're born a girl here, you have to do something to earn the respect that the boys already have." She'd add, before I even managed to open my mouth to complain, "There is no point in thinking about how fair or not that might be. You just have to do your part and hope to one day change it."

My aunt lived with us. Living with extended family is not unusual. Most Afghan households live in a system called Gad Kor. Gad Kor is a multi-family home with the sons of the same father living in the same compound. That system didn't extend to women, however. Once they married, they became footnotes to someone else's Gad Kor.

My aunt was a divorcée, and she lived with us because she had nowhere else to go. The man she married was outwardly a good match: he was educated, well-off, a respected lawyer. The moment that the door closed behind them after the wedding, however, the beatings started. Whenever she couldn't take it anymore, physically or mentally, she would come and live with us. As soon as she recovered, she would go back—not to him, but to her two children.

By the time the children were two and four, she couldn't take the abuse anymore. I was never told what happened, but one day she just stayed with us. There's nowhere for an Afghan woman in Pakistan to go. She was already a refugee, and you don't get to run twice over; there's not enough space left for that anymore.

My father took her in. He already lost one of his sisters to domestic violence—her husband beat her to death one day—and he wasn't going to risk losing another.

Divorce is not a woman-friendly affair in Pakistan, and leaving your husband almost always means losing access to your children.

Oh, my aunt fought and fought, and although everybody knew it was a useless fight, my family supported her through it. The kids stayed with the father, though, as they always do.

In Afghan households, children have free roam of the house. You can go sleep wherever you want—you don't even have to fake nightmares to secure a spot in your parents' bed. I spent most of my childhood happily sleeping in my parents' room; especially if my father's side was empty because he was either fighting in a war or sitting in prison. But when my aunt came, the entire household was rearranged. I was sent to sleep with her.

I suppose I was told to go sleep in her room so there would be a child breathing next to her as she lay awake, missing her own children. I found it hard to fall asleep there. She prayed most of the night, every night, night after night. Even at that age I knew what she was praying for.

If the beatings scarred her physically, leaving her children crushed my aunt's spirit. I always thought she looked mean: she was supernaturally thin—she couldn't eat or sleep; she was quick to anger and had unsettling eyes. It took growing up to realize that she was just broken.

I think we were all meant to make sure she was never alone with her thoughts. Being a teacher was not enough to keep her busy, so my father insisted that she go back to school to finish her master's degree. To my father, whatever the question, the answer was always education.

Most of the girls I knew in childhood were those who attended our school. Before that, other than my sister, my only company were my dreaded male cousins. Nour Bibi was the first girl I remember meeting. She was my mother's protégé—a math whiz, my mother always claimed. She, like so many Afghan girls, didn't have a happy home and kept lingering after classes at our place, postponing going home as long as she could. As my mother was already paying for all of her supplies and slipping her an allowance weekly, my mother decided to offer her the formal role of nanny.

Nour Bibi was slowly given chores, the allowance became an income, and hanging around became a job. It was a great source of pride for her. She would study in the corner of our living room, whenever she had free time, always present.

We were very little and needed help from Nour Bibi with everything. I still remember our daily struggles of putting shirts over my head and my arms into sleeves. I remember her as a shadow, as an outline. I have trouble remembering her face, but I could still draw her hands from memory as she was pushing shirts over my head.

Nour Bibi was the first woman in my life to disappear. She got married in her early teens, gone from one day to the next. We never heard from her again. It's like she ceased to exist.

Zarghona was our second nanny, this time chosen by our father. She was probably not the most obvious choice: the position entailed chasing three unruly children, and Zarghona was severely disabled and couldn't walk without her crutches, let alone run. She had polio as a child, and as a result, one of her legs completely atrophied. She couldn't walk for long, either, because the crutches would cut into her armpits until they bled.

Being a brat, I of course needed to know everything about it.

Does it hurt? (*Yes, it does.*)

Can she move it? (*No, she cannot.*)

After that, I'd retreat to my room to try to keep one leg steady while moving the other, curious to see what the world was like for Zarghona.

Despite all the fairly substantial disadvantages for the position of nanny, my father dug in his heels. He insisted that Zarghona was the kindest, most deserving candidate. We nodded agreeably, knowing that was only half the story. We all saw Zarghona's scars and we all knew she was beaten at home. My father was offering a refuge, not a job.

Zarghona was beaten almost daily, with savagery that isn't run of the mill. Every morning we'd see her come down the street to our house, limping slowly and crying over the latest bout of beatings and injuries. One of those mornings, when her father poured boiling water on her, Zarghona begged my mother to ask my father to intervene.

In our culture, it is beyond inappropriate to intervene in another family's affairs, even for a khan, no matter how obvious the scars or how difficult it may be to look away from them. Private is private. But as Zarghona's father worked for us, tending the vineyards, my father did go and threaten him with the loss of his job if he didn't stop beating Zarghona. I don't know if that helped. I don't remember any dramatic improvements in her situation.

There was something in all this that I found puzzling. Not the beatings—domestic violence behind closed doors is common, even us kids knew that. It was the fact that Zarghona lived with her mother, her stepmother, and three sisters and all of them were beaten daily. Six women beaten by a single man. I thought I had the solution and wondered why no one else thought of it: they could beat *him* up.

Once I voiced my avenger fantasy in front of Zarghona and my mother, there was stunned silence. Mistaking it for encouragement to continue speaking, I emphasized: "There are six of you!" My mother was still silent; my remark apparently was so exceedingly stupid and uniformed that it didn't even deserve a flying chaplak.

Suddenly, I was the one to pity.

"It's not how things work," Zarghona explained tiredly, assuming the role of a nanny.

"But why?" I insisted.

No one responded. They left it at that; neither felt the need to elaborate any further. It was the first of many times I've heard those words as way of explanation. Even all these years later, I still struggle to accept that as an answer. Things *could* work differently.

Maybe that's the worst part about being an Afghan woman: this resignation that comes with being beaten into submission. The abuse is so common that it becomes not only accepted, but acceptable. You don't fight back because you're never given a break. You're never given a chance to grow stronger.

Afghan children schedule school between chores, so school days are split into two: morning classes and evening classes. During the day, if you're a girl you're meant to help around the house. As a boy, you'd accompany your father to work, to a market or a field, whatever your father may do. I loved school, but my chores were light, and when it came to the afternoon classes, the choice was not between work and school, but between play and school. Guess which one I favored.

I was happy to go to school in the morning, I even enjoyed it, but evening classes really seemed unnecessary. I'd just get going with my digging when the yard would fill up with girls, all far more enthusiastic than me about going in. I'd have to be pulled out of the mud in the garden like a weed, kicking and screaming, told to clean up and attend classes.

My father picked a particularly school-obsessed girl to serve as a role model to me in those struggles: my namesake, The Other Pashtana, who—because of the endless praise bestowed upon her—quickly became my nemesis.

We played the same game almost every day. Sometimes it was my mother scolding me, sometimes my father, but the script was always the same: I'd be told to go to school, I would refuse, my father would immediately bring up the Other Pashtana and her willingness to be educated. The Other Pashtana, I was told, went to school happily, both in the morning and at night.

Eventually, I'd concede, muttering insults directed at the Other Pashtana, who was clearly to blame for all this. She was setting the wrong example. Had she been a normal girl who refused to go to school in the afternoon, we wouldn't have to have these conversations. How did they even know that she went willingly?

Truth be told, though, even I could see her eagerness.

In the summertime, she led a gaggle of girls to our door wondering if the school had started yet. They had no understanding of school holidays and didn't understand why the school would just randomly stop during the summer months. So they would show up at our door day after day looking for my aunt, demanding to be schooled. It went on for years, every summer. The Other Pashtana was in charge of knocking, and I was in charge of opening the door and explaining to them there was still no school. Nope, the summer is not over yet. Day after day.

I secretly enjoyed telling her she had to leave.

Her failure to grasp the concept of school holidays aside, she was one of those naturally smart kids. I was smart, but I always felt that was just because I spent so much studying, because my father was teaching me, because everybody around me pushed me toward learning. The Other Pashtana learned on her own. She was one of those annoyingly smart girls who just got things with seemingly no effort.

On top of all of that, she listened.

When the vaccine caravan came to the camp to vaccinate us against polio, my father had to herd all the people from the clan to our house. Yet, the effort it took to convince them to take the vaccine was nothing compared to the effort it took to convince me.

Once they tracked me down, which took hours, they forced me to take it. In Pakistan, the polio vaccine is administered orally, a vile-tasting liquid given by dropper into the mouth. I didn't want to swallow it but had no choice. However, as soon as they let go of me, I ran out in the garden and promptly tried to spit it out.

As I was scraping my tongue to get rid of the bitterness, who do I see when I look up but my father. He knew who he was dealing with. He took me by the hand and made me take the vaccine again.

After taking it a second time, I saw the Other Pashtana, the model child, who took the vaccine smilingly, without a complaint, being praised by all.

She had "Barbie hair," the most popular haircut in the camp that all of us wanted: bangs and waves, shoulder-length, lush and neat. Fake Barbie dolls were sold at every market, sitting next to the vegetables, but it wasn't really about the doll. It was the hair we all coveted, and the Other Pashtana had it. She was actually quite pretty. Her eyes, bright and kind, seemed to take up half her face, and although she was responsible for the best part of my daily misery, I liked being around her.

I went to her house often. Her family was one of the poorest around, and my aunt, who would always send food stuff to her students, would frequently send me to her house to drop something off. Yogurt, old clothes, or whatever extras we may have had.

The Other Pashtana's house was deep within the camp and had a squeaky, rusty green gate. Afghan houses, no matter how small and poor, normally have a courtyard area, an outer structure for receiving guests, and then the main house, divided in men's and women's quarters. Pashtana's mud house had none of that, only a curtain for the door and no place to receive guests. Inside, the kitchen wasn't divided into an area for bread making and cooking; all the walls were black because they cooked on open fire. You couldn't miss their poverty if you tried.

One day, the Other Pashtana didn't show up at school. My

father, at my insistence, went to their house to inquire what happened.

She wasn't going to go to school anymore; she got married, her father explained. Her new husband was a widower, in his late thirties, with three small children, and he needed someone to raise those children. Pashtana's father explained he had no choice but to marry her off because he couldn't feed her anymore. She would be better off this way, he said.

Pashtana was nine years old.

I knew about little girls getting married; it's everywhere around you, all these disappearing girls. But Pashtana was different. She was my measure of things, my ordering of the world. How could she be so easily erased? It was an end as final as death, without even being granted a funeral.

It was Pashtana who made me want to change things.

We didn't talk about her anymore in our house. I stopped complaining about school. I went morning and evening, studying for both of us. To a far less tragic and brutal extent, her marriage made me grow up too.

I've never seen her again, and to this day, Pashtana feels like an unfinished conversation.

I wish I had a way to let her know that I still remember her. That I'm sorry.

3

NOT ONE OF MY FAMILY MEMBERS IS OLD ENOUGH to have memories of Afghanistan at peace. Being a Afghan doesn't do much for your longevity; in addition to the never-ending war, we also have tribal feuds that further diminish your odds of a long life. I lost seven of my cousins to various blood feuds.

Our community may have fled the war, but no one left their weapons behind. There were always guns around us: Kalashnikovs, rifles, AK-47s; you learn young to differentiate between them, by sound and by sight.

I first held a gun when I was seven. Tomboy or not, a girl playing with weapons was too much even for my parents, so I was kept away from them. However, my father was always armed, even around the house. There were too many enemies to ever put the gun down. But one day, he apparently did. I spotted my father's 9mm on the windowsill in the living room. No one was around and I clearly had to pick it up. I climbed up to the window and got it. I understood it wasn't safe, so I quickly put it back down. But in doing so, I somehow unhooked the safety, and the gun went off the next time my father picked it up. People frequently get hurt with weapons that accidentally discharge, and everybody has a story of a cousin that got killed or maimed by way of a stray bullet. Thankfully, no one was hurt that day, but the event did cause a bit of a ruckus. Grown-ups talked about it for days, some going as far as suggesting a conspiracy. I was horrified but never admitted to my father it was me. It traumatized me sufficiently not to pick up a gun again, though.

When I was twelve, we had to flee our home in the middle of the night because of a tribal dispute. There was a car accident involving a member of our family which killed a man from another clan. The other family insisted that he was pushed off the road.

Pashtun clans are like the musketeers: one for all and all for one, which sounds great until you find yourself being held responsible for something you haven't done. If one person from your clan offends in any way a person from another clan, it can start an open season on all the clan members. My father may not have been anywhere near the road where the accident happened—let alone driving the car—but as a khan, as the leader, he was likely their first target.

There is a way out of it, of course, called "blood money." It's our culture's equivalent of paying damages. We offered to pay, but once the other family refused to accept money, fleeing was the only thing left to do. It took a whole year before things settled down and before we could return to the camp.

We fled to Karachi. I was homeschooled there, partly because we all knew it was temporary and there was little point in settling, and partly to keep me safe. Being "homeschooled" meant only that I studied at home: there was no program, no curriculum to follow. It was just me and my beloved Encarta.

I don't know if anyone still remembers what Encarta was: a digital encyclopedia that you'd get on a disk, containing answers to whatever question you could think of. When they shut it down in 2009, I mourned it like it was a family member taken in its prime.

That year in Karachi, I would methodically read everything Encarta had to offer, taking notes as I went. History was by far my favorite subject. I covered everything, from Alexander the Great to the Soviets. I felt like I was furthering my learning immensely, like I was cracking the core of all knowledge. I was learning rapidly, but without any direction. It was like trying to learn a language by reading a dictionary. At the end of that year, I was full of facts and ideas which, as I was about to find out, no one in the school system cared about.

When the tribal dispute was finally settled and we went back to the camp, my parents enrolled me in a top private school in Quetta, hoping to make up for lost time. It was not a place that appreciated autodidacts. My deep but scattered general knowledge was deemed insufficient. I learned differently, I thought differently, and behaved differently.

It was a disaster.

I was the only Afghan there in a sea of rich Pakistani girls. I was the only one in the entire school wearing a headscarf. My father would show up for parent-teacher conferences in his traditional Kandahari robes, with a turban to top it off. He would wait his turn to see my teachers, surrounded by Pakistani doctors and lawyers wearing suits. It was an expensive, prestigious private school attended by the Pakistani elites. An Afghan leader with a chubby daughter was no one's idea of a suitable fit. No one was willing to look beyond the fact that we looked different. No one even tried.

Life at school was like a bootleg version of *Mean Girls* with Urdu subtitles.

Bullying was hardly new to me; courtesy of my male cousins, I developed an extraordinarily thick skin. Yet this was something else entirely. It was not only the students. That I probably could have ignored. It was the contempt and racism of the teachers that broke me. In a passive-aggressive way, with that colonial attitude that the Pakistani upper classes so cherish, it was suggested to me that this perhaps was "not my cup of tea." The tea they were talking about was education in general and my upcoming O Levels, in particular. O Levels in Pakistan are a standardized exam that is academically optional, but necessary as a status symbol, as it often signifies a desire to eventually study abroad. My teachers didn't see the reason for me to take the test. Their attitude had nothing to do with my grades or aptitude. As far as they were concerned, I was already well above my station in life attending their precious school. I had no place asking for more. They repeated it so often even I started to doubt myself.

It was an Afghanistan-heavy day when it all came to a head. By accident or by design, we had several classes in which we would be learning about my country. You'd think I'd look forward to it given how much I loved the subject. Instead, I had this feeling of foreboding.

Geography was first.

The teacher kept pointedly looking at me as he berated my country. How barren it is. Such bad topography. That's the real reason people are fleeing that country. It's just a pile of rocks. I shuffled in my seat, and I kept biting my tongue, and I somehow got through it.

But the day wasn't over yet.

It was the Islamic Studies class next. Our teacher was a respected scholar, but one of those closeted armchair jihadists. That day, he decided to share with the class his views on the war in Afghanistan as he sat in his comfortable chair, never having had to bury anyone killed in a war.

I don't remember his arguments all that clearly other than that they were dismissive, prejudiced, and wrong: I'd already reached my limit with the "piles of rocks" comment in geography class and was struggling to keep quiet. I don't remember my own argument very clearly either, other than that it started with, "How dare you?"

Everybody knows that nothing good comes after that sentence.

It got me suspended from school for three days, and although my outburst changed little, it felt like it was worth it. Speaking up wasn't about any burning desire to dip my toes into shark-infested Pakistani politics, but rather a public declaration that I just won't be bullied. It was my very first act of public dissent.

In many ways, my activism was inevitable. Tribal people like me lived on the social periphery of the Pakistani state. Pashtuns and Balochs, the minority tribes, were at best ignored, and at worst, actively persecuted. Add to it being a refugee—and a girl—and you find yourself always being seen as less than. I didn't want to be less than. I wanted the right to occupy space, to have a voice. I didn't think those were outrageous demands.

My father stood by me. Turbaned or not, he was a calm, eloquent, educated man, and a good person to defend a hotheaded, foul-mouthed daughter in a school setting. It helped somewhat, him going in, talking to them and offering articulate arguments as to why they should keep political views out of school. It wasn't enough, though. It was the system, not just the people there, and a single meeting with school officials wasn't going to change that. Little, if anything improved. We all knew I was there on borrowed time.

To top it all off, puberty wasn't kind to me. I seemed to have been expanding sideways, not upward, so when stress started to cause me to lose weight, I wasn't entirely displeased. But when I started losing my hair, there was no positive spin I could put on it. My hair was falling out in fistfuls, and I had several bald spots. It was getting to be too much. I was not going to give up on education, we all knew that, but the school, once my sanctuary, now felt like it was going to be the end of me.

As I was already attending the best school in Quetta, switching to any other school there would have been a step down. Worse, it would have been seen as *them* being right all along, with their cups of tea and the perpetual bullying. Unwilling to even contemplate that, I looked at schools outside the city. There was a school in Lahore, even more rigorous than this one, but it seemed somehow nicer. It's not like they advertised *Mean Girls* in the brochures for the Quetta school, but the Lahore school had smiling girls on the front page. What a novel concept, I thought.

I didn't really have to explain much why I needed to leave: my parents saw what was going on. It all seemed logical under the circumstances, even to them. Still, leaving your family at age fourteen to go study in another city, away from one's parents, was unheard of. Even for boys, let alone a girl. As usual, I left it to my father to defend it to the myriad of uncles that strenuously objected to it.

"You're sending her away? She's going to find someone and marry and run away, never even finishing her studies!"

Or: "Why spend all that money on a girl? She'll marry and all that money will be wasted. What's worse, someone else will benefit from it."

That's a cardinal sin by Pashtun standards, by the way. You're meant to go through life hoping the neighbor's cow would die before you prayed for the health of your own. As far as the rest of the family was concerned, not only was my father taking away the money from his son, but he was indirectly allowing someone else to profit. I never said we were perfect.

My father stood his ground, however.

Once I got to Lahore it became clear the girls in the brochure were paid to smile. The school was even more demanding than the one I left. The atmosphere was friendlier, though. Maybe it was because no one had enough time to bully; they buried us in homework.

The school didn't offer boarding, and I lived in a private women's dorm that was within walking distance to my school, populated with medical students in their twenties. They were kind and cared for me as much as they could, but no one had time to play family with me; they had their own studies to worry about. Too scared and shy to go out by myself, I rarely left the dorm. I studied twelve, sometimes fourteen hours a day. It wasn't just about being driven; there was so little else for me to do.

My social life revolved around social media: namely, Facebook. I know people in the developed world don't necessarily associate Facebook with Pashtun teens, but technologically, we don't differ that much from our peers elsewhere. We may not have rfunctional independent governments, but most of us do have phones. It's sometimes easy to forget that Egypt started a revolution on Facebook, that India started the riots. Pakistan wasn't that different. Teens used it to stay in touch, but for all, Facebook was a place to get updates on family and air your political grievances.

I'd venture out only to go to university fairs. I loved university fairs. I'd go there to daydream, to steel myself with hope. In my mind, the line between being uneducated and being educated felt like a physical border to cross. A degree was the passport to the other side, where life was less brutal, less chaotic than the one in camp. I knew that education doesn't make you immune to discrimination, but I knew in my heart that it protected you from the worst of it. Every time I came back from the fair, there were new brochures to put in a file, like souvenirs from travel.

The Oxford one proudly sat on top of them all.

When I wasn't studying, I read. On my nightstand there were only biographies. They served partly as inspiration, but also as concrete maps to an uncharted territory. Although my family was highly educated by anyone's standards, let alone the camp's dwellers, their advanced degrees were almost ornamental. My father, despite his master's in communications, was a tribal leader, never transcending his traditional role. I was meant to be the first one to push the boundaries. My degree was meant to lead to a *career*. I didn't necessarily know back then which career that might be, but the simple idea of having a choice was thrilling enough.

On a good day, I was willing to accept the sacrifices it required. As torturous and lonely as these school years were, they would surely eventually pay off. I kept reminding myself that Mandela had to stay in prison for twenty-nine years, and I'd only been miserable for about two. I had no right to complain, I was too young for that.

Mandela was and still is my idol. He's the only one I knew of that managed to reconcile the idea of a tribe and a country. The modern world sees caring for your community, for your tribe, as something to overcome on the way to becoming a modern country. Not Mandela. He refused to pack light and leave his tribal values by the side of the road. He didn't think it was necessary to undo old structures before building new ones. For him, a tribe was a building block.

I understood the clash of tribal and modern well. Having always gone to city schools, many of them UN funded, my curriculum was all western and chock-full of stories of human rights and equality. The moment I stepped out of the school, however, those rights were nowhere to be seen. Instead, I was surrounded by battered women, and child marriage, and literacy rates that never seem to go above 50 percent.

Yet our code, our culture is so much more than the sum of these failings. Mandela proved that there was more than one template, that we don't have to look outward for direction to make things around us better. Like any other system, tribal values can evolve too. We don't have to adopt another culture completely, become unrecognizable to ourselves to fit in with the rest of the world. Mandela was the only person who understood that, or maybe the only one brave enough to try.

I had lesser saints, too, the ones that were deeply personal: Martin Luther King Jr. "and Bacha Khan," who inspired my activism for Pashtun rights. The idea of nonviolence always resonated as an alternative to our gun-toting attitudes.

I worshiped Indira Gandhi, the first Indian woman prime minister. The whole idea of Oxford came from her. It was an almost unhealthy obsession; there are parts of her biography I can still probably recite by heart. You'd think it was because of all her achievements, and to an extent, yes, of course it was. But what I loved about her the most was that she felt human to me: failing her Latin exams, struggling with being less than perfect. Freshly out of that school in Quetta, finding out that even Indira Gandhi had her own not-your-cup-of-tea issues before eventually leading India was all the encouragement I needed.

I was also obsessed with Benazir Bhutto, the first female prime minister of Pakistan. Clearly, not for her politics—she's the one that made the Taliban what they are—but as a woman, she fascinated me to no end. I remember when they blew her up. I remember the shock that the country felt, the sense of fear.

I tried not to dwell too much on the fact that both of my heroines ended up in a pool of blood.

It was in that dorm room in Lahore that I started writing about political issues in a slightly more organized fashion, partly because I was alone and had no family near me to listen to my endless rants. At first, I posted my opinions on social media, but I quickly graduated to submitting op-eds to Afghan papers. I'd concentrate on two issues that I knew best and understood firsthand: education of girls and refugee rights.

You'd think no one would care what some teen girl had to say, but military regimes have fragile egos: they need everyone to agree with them. It didn't matter who I was—although being a girl was adding an insult to injury; it was my gall to speak up that bothered them. The Afghan Taliban, attached to the Pakistani military's hip, started noticing, too. I didn't quite realize just how much they disliked what I had to say until they tried to blow me up a few years later.

It was toward the end of the school year that I woke up with a sharp pain in my stomach. I skipped school and called my mother. No matter what hurts, my mother always blames indigestion. You could have lost your arm and a leg, and she'd still be advising you to take fiber. Predictably, indigestion was the first word out of her mouth. When the pain intensified, she told me to drink milk with Sprite, an Afghan, off-brand version of Mylanta.

Nothing helped. The pain wasn't subsiding, and having exhausted my mother's arsenal of indigestion remedies, it became obvious, even on a long-distance call, that I required medical attention. That's when my father stepped in, calling in favors from friends to come get me and drive me to the hospital. Once we got to the ER, the doctor told me my appendix was at the point of bursting. He explained that if left untreated, it was likely going to kill me. He directed me to go get a number and wait my turn to go into surgery.

Pakistani hospitals don't prioritize surgeries by urgency. Unless you're important, unless you know someone or bribe someone, you're meant to join a long line of people that were there before you. As an Afghan girl of fifteen on her own in a Pakistani medical facility, I was not the hospital's highest priority. This was clear looking at the number I was given; there were over three hundred surgeries before they could get to me. It could be days before they'd get to operate on me. According to the doctor, I had hours at best, and the chances of me surviving the wait were not very high.

Dying at fifteen, alone in a Pakistani waiting room, was not how I was going to go, I decided. It was time for me to call my father again, and for him to call another friend, this time, the one with the connections instead of a car. In a matter of minutes, his friend magically managed to clear over three hundred people off that list and they scooped me off the floor where I was lying bent in pain and rushed me in to operate.

I woke up alone. There was no one there to greet me, to be happy that I survived. My father was on his way, but he had to make sure I got into surgery before he could hop on a flight to Lahore, so it was going to be a while.

As soon as my father arrived, he took me home to Quetta to recover. I was still drugged, and for once couldn't argue, but I insisted on going back to do the exams as soon as I was able to stand up again. I don't know that there was a real need for me to return for those exams, but lying in that hospital bed all alone made me realize the full extent of the sacrifices we all made for my education, and I couldn't let all of that be for nothing. This was just the latest hurdle, and I stopped counting them a while ago. To postpone finishing that year, even for health reasons, just wasn't an option.

But all this travelling back and forth wasn't a good idea post-surgery. You're not even meant to walk after it, and it was too much for my fresh stitches. Sitting in my classroom in Lahore taking my exams, I could feel them separating, I could feel the infection setting in, I was feeling feverish, but I ignored it. I sat taking the year-end exams, for several hours, with a wound bleeding through my shirt. When I got up, the entire front of my shirt was stained bright red. I needed medical attention again, but I passed the exams.

When the news of my post-surgery exam drama spread around the family, one of my uncles, who, like everybody else was initially against me being sent to Lahore, called my father. "You better support her now until the day she dies. She has to stay in school. If she cares this much, you should never take it away. I hope you know that." Pashtuns don't admit—ever—that they're wrong. To this day, my uncle is the only one I know.

The rest of my time in Lahore was uneventful in comparison. I started sending applications out to different universities. With each application I sent I'd try to imagine what my life would be like if I went there. The second round of applications was for scholarships for each of the universities. I applied for the Oxford preparatory program, filling out endless forms, writing essays that were meant to convince them that some refugee brat is worth their attention and their money. Oxford always held a special meaning. Oxford, more than any other place, held the promise of a career, of breaking the mold.

There was an odd choice in all these applications: I applied to the American University of Afghanistan in Kabul. It was hardly an academically driven decision. My father promised to take me to Afghanistan, so to make sure he made good on his promise, I registered for the English proficiency test in Kandahar, as well as the entrance exam to the American University of Afghanistan. The tests were a day apart, and there's no better insurance that a trip would actually happen than attaching an educational event to it. My father would have no choice but to take me.

But the closer I was to getting to Oxford, the closer I was getting to achieving my dream, the more the dream seemed insubstantial and somewhat frivolous. I spent my afternoons reading biographies of leaders who attended that fabled institution, but I spent my nights missing our school at home, thinking about all the girls from the camp that couldn't read or write and then simply disappeared.

The more I thought about it, the more it seemed to me that it all starts with education. Lack of education wasn't a byproduct of poverty; it was a weapon. Denying it was deliberate and served a political purpose. It was meant to keep the girls silent, compliant, and disconnected from the world. It denied them a voice. My op-eds became more forceful. The responsibility was on us, on educated Afghans, to change it. We owe the illiterate a debt, I insisted.

Advocating for girls' education made me an equal opportunity offender: challenging both the tribal notions of propriety and Pakistan's treatment of us. I was endearing myself to no one, my extended family included.

"What business does she have talking about other people's children? Criticizing the ways that other girls are brought up? Those girls have fathers! Who does she think she is?"

My father's support for me made it possible to ignore the dissenting voices, but it still didn't answer my main question: What exactly was I supposed to do? If helping these disappearing girls was the point, where did Oxford fit in, really?

I thought of the Other Pashtana, lost forever, to me and to the world. I thought of all the other girls like her. I'd lie awake in bed thinking how to reach those girls. How to teach them their rights, how to teach them what they needed to know to survive. Thriving would be nice, yes, but how do you define your goals when even survival is uncertain? What constitutes education for people who know nothing of the world other than guns and dying?

I was home for the holidays, in a house full of guests, when the letter for the preparatory program in Oxford came. I opened it in private, breathless with excitement. I was accepted! It took a while to take it in, and although my mother was in the next room, I first called my father who was away on business. I wanted to let him know, I wanted to confirm one more time, now that this was real, that I could go. Once he said yes, only then did I run to my mother and tell her.

That day, all the sacrifices, all the arguments seemed to have paid off. My trajectory angered so many in our family, but none of that mattered now. Oxford!

My mother chose not to celebrate for too long, concentrating on what's truly important instead: burning sage for protection from the evil eye, from jealousy that could cause me bad luck. The house reeked of sage for days. Never the one to miss her prayer time, she now prayed for me with an intensity I hadn't seen before.

I was elated. It was an achievement; I knew it was.

All I needed to do now was tell them I didn't want to go.

4

THE EXCITEMENT ABOUT THE OXFORD PROGRAM lingered in the household for weeks, along with the scent of sage, but I was already fixating on something else: seeing Afghanistan for the first time. My father was taking me to Kandahar so I could take the English proficiency test which was a prerequisite for every university program I applied to. Since we were going to be in Afghanistan anyway, I would also take the entrance exam for American University in Kabul. After all, we had paid for it already, and somehow it seemed less of a waste if I actually took it, even if wasn't going to the school.

My father planned our visit for weeks. Sangeena, my sister, decided to come with us, for the fear of missing out, no doubt. The trip meant so much more than just a few days away from home. We were going home. My sister and I could barely contain ourselves.

As soon as we crossed the border, everything seemed different. The line that divides Pakistan from Afghanistan may have been imaginary once, but it's been there long enough and the moment you cross it, you enter a different world.

It felt familiar, like a longing finally satisfied, a longing you never knew you had. It was home. The air smelled somehow different, maybe because the land was tilled and not just poked with sticks to keep refugee tents in place.

Still, our first impressions were hardly favorable. Once on Afghan soil, we seemed to be surrounded by a sea of blue burqas. Sangeena gasped loudly, as she often did for dramatic effect, every time she saw a woman covered from head to toe. I may have kept quiet, but I was shocked, too.

My father quickly grew impatient: "It's a rural area. Burqas tell you nothing. You have to learn to see beyond burqas." It was a reprimand. A deserved one, too, I realized. Who were we to be shocked by their traditional garb? I thought back to being the only girl with a headscarf at school in Quetta. I thought of my father in his turban at parent-teacher conferences. I finally understood how out of place we must have appeared to everyone. It hurt me to admit it, even to myself, but it seemed like I wasn't immune to judging either.

But something else stood out to me: covered or not, there were more women milling around than I've ever seen in the camp in Pakistan.

I also noticed that the roads were actually better than I had expected. I don't know what I thought they would be like—crater after crater? more of a mountaineering expedition than a drive? — but while there was plenty of damage all around us, the road itself was not too bad. I've seen bumpier.

We weren't going to go far that first day: just to Spin Boldak, a border town, the place where my father almost died. We were going to stay with a distant relative, a man who used to work for my father at the beginning of the war.

Arrival there was anticlimactic, to say the least: the place was completely, utterly, mind-numbingly boring. Of course, we were not to show it. My father may tolerate rebellion, but rudeness was inexcusable.

He soon left to visit his other friends in town while my sister and I stayed behind with our hosts. They were glued to a cricket match.

Cricket is immensely popular, both in Pakistan and in Afghanistan, but it's definitely an acquired taste. Games take hours, even days. Our hosts weren't watching the game, which would have been bad enough. They were listening to it on a radio. A radio commentary takes the cricket experience to a whole new level. I thought I could feel my brain cells dying. There was a girl about my age there, our host's sister Durdana, but there was no talking during the game, so that hardly mattered. We just sat there, wilting away, occasionally woken up from our stupor by what, to us, seemed like random boos and cheers.

The sunset finally put us out of our misery, and as we retreated to the women's quarters, I finally got a chance to talk to Durdana. We struggled with a conversation, maybe because neither one of us said a word all day, and maybe because we had so little in common. Still, I could tell that there was something she wanted to say to me. It wasn't due to my superior perception skills; she literally ambushed me as I exited the bathroom. There was clearly something she wanted to discuss.

My father mentioned before we arrived that Durdana's mother died of cancer when she was very young. The term "cancer" wasn't necessarily a diagnosis in Afghanistan. It was a catch-all illness that meant someone died before his time without being struck by a bullet. Dying is divided into violent or nonviolent deaths here: the nonviolent death was always labeled as cancer: it could be malnutrition, heart attack or actual cancer, but if you didn't get killed by a bullet or a bomb, everybody would just call it cancer. We had to so carefully explore and organize our violent deaths that there was little patience left for differentiating between the illnesses.

Durdana was interested in medicine. "I'd like to become a doctor one day, I think. My mother, you know . . ."

"I know," I said, "I know." I didn't want her to have to explain her mother's death. "Medicine, ha? That's a lot of studying." My conversations somehow always end up being discussions about education, and it rarely takes long to arrive at the subject. Unexpectedly, that turned out to be exactly what Durdana wanted to talk about. "I read your articles," she said. "I also follow your posts on social media. I always 'Like' your posts on girls' education. And I do study a lot. But there's no school for girls in Spin Boldak, so it's hard."

"How do you do it?" I asked.

"My brother helps sometimes; he teaches me stuff he learned in school. But he's older and he has to work. I just do what I can, by myself."

Durdana disappeared for a moment and came back from her room with a stack of papers. She proudly showed me rows and rows of letters she was printing. She used the four-line paper, like a first grader just learning how to write. "Want me to show you?" She was clearly proud of her work. Then, she picked up a pencil.

That was the moment that broke my heart. Durdana held a pencil as if it were a delicate porcelain teacup, with two fingers, clumsily and hesitantly, so utterly at odds with her determination.

I was born left-handed. From my earliest days, my studies included learning to write in Arabic, and writing with a left hand was considered *haram*, forbidden, so I had to switch to my right hand. When I was little, they'd take a pencil from my left hand and place it in my right, where it didn't fit, where letters came out crooked and uneven no matter how hard I tried. That's how Durdana wrote at the age of sixteen.

It seemed inconsiderate and impolite to express the intense anger that rose up within me. In our little school in the house, learning to write was one of the first fundamental skills the girls were taught. I thought I knew how much our school meant to our community, but you never really see the full picture until you meet someone who doesn't have access to it. Watching Durdana pick up a pencil was the moment when my dream of Oxford slipped away.

She and I stayed up into the night, printing block letters, trying to find a way to get her into school, any school. I gave her the tablet I had—she hadn't seen one before. "There's a whole curriculum on the internet. It can help you a lot. And I will help you, too," I promised.

In the morning, as we were leaving, she hugged me as tightly as she could without letting go of the tablet that I gave her. She needed it far more than I did. She was holding on to me as if her one hope was about to walk out the door. I promised myself not to let her down.

AS WE DROVE TOWARD KANDAHAR CITY, MY FATHER KEPT TRYING TO give us a guided tour of the province and the war. He pointed to the lands that belonged to our tribe and our family. He explained where stories that we grew up hearing about took place.

"This is where we fought with the Taliban."

"This is where we starved for eight days."

"This is where the Americans would air-drop money."

It was like adding illustrations to the storybook of his life.

Still, I kept interrupting his stories with questions about Durdana.

"You should write an angry letter to the governor and demand they open a school in Spin Boldak. Will you do that?"

My father nodded and continued: "Now, this road—"

"Father," I interrupted again, "you should have seen her! She's practically illiterate. She can't print letters, but she's all over social media on her phone, demanding the government should open a school! I am going to help her."

I wanted my father's reassurance that Durdana would be included in the flock of girls that have been helped by my family over the years. And although I would be the one to drive the change this time around, goodwill wasn't going to be enough. I needed money—his, obviously—not much, but some. She needed textbooks, she needed pencils and papers. I was determined that Durdana should get the education she so wanted. I'd help her learn. Somehow, I'd help her.

It was unfathomable to me. It made me so angry. She seemingly had everything in place: willingness to learn, support of the family, and, still, she couldn't get educated.

I let out all my anger, everything I held in for fear of offending her, and unleashed it on the unsuspecting, unprepared audience in the car. I wanted to *do* something about it.

With the full force of my innate stubbornness, and with that angry righteousness of a teen, I demanded that the system be changed, preferably before we reached Kandahar.

They waited out my tirade, as they often did, and my father finally said what he'd always said to me: "You'll figure it out."

That never failed to shut me up.

As you approach Kandahar city from the direction of Spin Boldak, you approach it like an advancing army trying to take over the city: by way of the prison. Afghans may be somewhat lacking when it comes to punishing crime, but political opposition hadn't been tolerated for years, and the prisons were always full of political prisoners.

Before any takeover, the race to save them would start as soon as the countryside fell into new hands. The losing army would try to execute as many prisoners as possible before retreating, getting rid of potential fighters now that the tide had turned.

When my father entered the city fighting against the Taliban, they too followed the tradition. The first battle was the one for the prison. He told us about the people they freed, the strange air of last-minute pardons they had about them: disbelief, relief, and the will to fight.

I learned only later that my uncle was one of those granted a stay of execution that day. The Taliban had him scheduled to die the following morning, and by the time he heard the sounds of the gun battle in his cell, he had already made peace with dying. He said his prayers, he was ready, but when the doors of the cell opened, instead of the Taliban taking him to his execution, it was a group of men headed by my father.

I don't know why my father skipped over that story on our drive in; maybe he deemed it too much reality for the first trip to Afghanistan. It is also possible that he just didn't want to claim his cousin's story as his own. It was his brother who had to get ready to die, my father just opened the door of the cell. My father was the kind of man that would leave the telling of that story to the person who survived it.

Once we entered Kandahar, my father said little. My sister and I were uncharacteristically speechless as well. Kandahar is a mesmerizing, beautiful place, a transplant from a different time. You'd expect everything to be in ruins, but what greets you as you enter the city are beautiful palaces and flowers. There are flowers everywhere.

In later years I would fly over Kandahar and see that it is all dusty and brown from above, but when you walk through it, it feels alive and full of color. It was the Afghanistan of Khan Bibi, intact, real.

I was somewhat skeptical of those stories before. Being a refugee makes you an unreliable witness to your own losses and things that you left behind. But there it was, in its full glory, lying in front of me. I remember there were roses blooming in December. In December!

Kandaharis love their flowers. They know all there is about gardening, and often their garden is the first thing they show their visitors. Not the house, but the garden. It's a connection to the land, as if the house is something they only temporarily inhabit, and the land is what constitutes a home.

My tribe, the Durranis, has never been nomadic. Our whole existence is a long, stubborn effort to return to the land.

We pulled up at the place where we were staying. It belonged to one of our cousins, and it was a giant, empty palace. Not a mansion, an actual palace, plucked out of fairy tales. But for all its beauty, there was no water, no electricity—and it was colder than any indoor place I had ever been to. It had the most intricate silk curtains, the most beautiful carpets, yet it was as cold and dark and drafty as an alleyway in the middle of a bitter winter.

Sangeena promptly had a panic attack: "This is all fake! Nothing is working here. I'm going to die here." I said nothing. I just kept looking around, thinking what a perfect setting this would be for a horror movie. It was one of those places where you walk in and just know that nothing good can happen there. It was impossible for either one of us to reconcile the beauty of the place with the lack of amenities. It was a drafty, empty shell, forgotten in time.

As we settled in for the night, I learned that Hafiz, a friend of mine since childhood who had moved to Kabul, had died that day. He was murdered by the Taliban. They entered the house and started shooting. They killed one of the younger children first and then got Hafiz as he was trying to get the rest of the kids to safety. Hafiz was only starting his life—he had just gotten engaged, just graduated. His family was from a different province—Oruzgan— but we belonged to the same tribe. They left Pakistan a few years ago.

My very first night in Afghanistan, and a close friend got killed in a daytime attack in the middle of Kabul. Grief alternated with fear. I started to think coming to Afghanistan was a terrible idea. As far as omens go, Hafiz's death wasn't a good one.

I was already fearful and uncertain about my direction, and this made it all worse. Sangeena, on the other hand, definitely didn't lack certainty. To my sister, being in Afghanistan meant only one thing: we were all going to die. Or rather, *I* would die because she had no intention of staying in this godforsaken country any longer than necessary: "Why would you even think of coming here? They murdered Hafiz, so they will definitely murder you. And he was nice, you're not. You never keep your mouth shut. They will definitely kill *you*."

I cried into my pillow as my sister kept praying into the morning for the test site not to be attacked while I was there, for me not to die in Afghanistan. She prayed grudgingly, as if asking God to protect me from my own stupidity. She did so loudly, trying to drown out the fear in her head.

I barely got any sleep, and the next morning, puffy-eyed and already in a bad mood, I had to wait for her to get ready. I was going to take the test that would decide my future. I needed to pass it in order to pursue any future education; every acceptance was conditioned by it. But my sister refused to wash with cold water and refused to leave without having washed first. Our house, like most big houses in Kandahar, came with the guards with ancient Kalashnikovs that were borderline antiques. In Afghanistan, an outpost that housed them was an amenity, like an extra bathroom in a real estate listing. The guards were now summoned inside and, along with my father, started the interminable process of heating up water over an open fire. I was fuming.

When we finally got on our way, I hoped the drama was over, but no: Sangeena refused to get out of the car when we arrived. This time around, even I balked. It wasn't the threat of imminent death anymore, but I could definitely see her point. Kandahar isn't exactly the most popular place to take your exams unless you actually live there. There was a long line of girls entering the hotels where the test was taking place, and every single girl walking in was fully covered, wearing a burqa.

In comparison, my sister and I looked positively indecent. I rocked my kali: loose pants and long shirt and scarf that covered my hair but nowhere as tightly, nowhere as completely as their hair was tucked out of sight. I started getting flashbacks to the *Mean Girls* of Quetta—yet again I stood out. I thought being back in Afghanistan would make me belong. That it wouldn't require any effort to fit in. I could not have been more wrong, and this was just a glimpse of things to come.

When I walked into the building, I got the same treatment I got in Pakistani schools. I couldn't find my pencil to fill out a form and tried to borrow one, but everyone looked past me, and not one of them responded.

It was the first time I realized that being a refugee, that growing up elsewhere, means to be viewed as a stranger wherever you go. You're an Afghan in Pakistan, and a Pakistani in Afghanistan. You can self-define all you want, but you belong nowhere.

I always default to fight, though. Being ignored only strengthened my resolve. I do well when odds are against me, I develop some sort of spiteful tunnel vision. Don't knock spite as a driving force. All of a sudden I wasn't tired from my sister's all-night praying session. I wasn't devastated by the grief of losing Hafiz. I walked in and aced that test. And then I aced the second one. And I knew it.

In the afternoon, our father took us sightseeing with a running commentary that served as a subtle reminder that no one can take away your home: not the invading armies, not the disapproving looks.

My father's stories invariably had a military bent: "For the past three hundred years, as soon as Kandahar fell, the rest of the country went with it; it was only a matter of time. Outsiders look to Kabul for answers, because it's the capital, but Afghans know that our tea leaves are read in Kandahar. If you rule there, the country is yours for the taking. Kandahar is where all of our history starts, our country's and our family's."

Sangeena and I nodded in unison as he said it. It's the story he'd been telling us for as long as we both could remember. We come from two long and respected tribal lines, and we knew that Kandahar's history and that of our family were intertwined. To prove it, my father decided that our first stop would be the Ahmad Shah tomb. Considered the founder of modern Afghanistan, Ahmad Shah Durrani also founded a dynasty that ruled Afghanistan for centuries. Like most Afghans, Sangeena and I knew well who he was—we Afghans referred to him as Ahmad Shah Baba, "Ahmad Shah Our Father"—and we could recite both his military victories and his poems. My father talked about him so often, it felt like Ahmad Shah had a seat at our dinner table.

Sangeena finally got out of the car when we got to the Durrani mausoleum, Ahmad Shah Baba Ziarat. My father, although not overly religious, disappeared into the Shrine of the Cloak to pray. It's adjacent to the tomb and houses one of the holiest relics in Islam, the cloak supposedly worn by the prophet Mohammed on his night journey. The cloak is taken out only in times of great peril for Afghanistan, and few are allowed to pray there. My father, because he was a tribal leader, was one of those few.

We waited outside the mausoleum while our father prayed. The solemnity and wonder of it all were soon gone. We ran around like two giggly schoolgirls, which is really what we were. My sister's enthusiasm is as infectious as her sulking, and so we took selfie after selfie, posing and grinning outside all Kandahar's monuments. We wanted to show our country to everybody back home: "Look how safe! Look how beautiful!"

I'm not a forgiving kind, though, and I was still set on getting my sister back for her earlier petulance and insults. When we got back to that not-so-little house of horrors, my father had to go for a meeting, and we were left alone in that empty house with the guards outside. It was cold, so we huddled in bed with a computer perched on the covers, ready to watch a movie.

My sister wanted a romantic comedy, and I said I knew just the one. I showed her the picture on the front—it was Al Pacino, who, she'd decided, was definitely handsome enough for the lead, looking like a Bollywood star. "And he's a refugee in a movie, too!" I kept selling.

With that, we sat down and watched *Scarface*.

Of course, I knew what the movie was about: cocaine and

murders and blood and violence. It's a Cuban version of Pashtun except with different drugs. I knew my sister wouldn't leave the bed. It was a strange, big house and her choices were limited: she could either stay with me and watch it, or she could go be by herself in a scary, empty house. Sangeena never moved. She spent most of the movie shrieking and covering her eyes, but she never moved.

It was payback for having to wait for her in the morning to get ready, for her praying so loudly that I couldn't sleep the night before my test, for telling me they'd kill me, for making me afraid.

And also, I just loved Al Pacino, and I really needed a break.

When my father returned, as soon as Sangeena heard the door open and before he'd even entered the room, she was already telling on me, crying on cue: "Pashtana made me watch *Scarface*! They're all dead! And there was blood! There was blood everywhere!" Sangeena then started sobbing so violently it was difficult to understand what she was saying, but the theme of death and destruction was clear to all.

My father looked tired, but nevertheless took the time to scold me: "What were you thinking, Pashtana? Traumatizing a child like that?"

I may have even pretended out of respect to care as he yelled. But that night, I slept like a baby.

5

WITH THE EXAMS OVER, WE NOW HAD TIME TO visit all our cousins in Kandahar city. The area where they lived seemed untouched by the fighting. But if the facades of the buildings didn't show the scars of war, the damage it caused was in full view once you entered the households. Every house we visited, rich or poor, had orphans and widows taken in by the family members. The real suffering was—as always seems to be the case in Afghanistan—hidden behind closed doors.

The first stop on the family tour was to visit my great-uncle, who lived in yet another mansion that made anyone who entered feel like a poor, provincial cousin. They had a wedding in the house recently. Afghan weddings go on for days, sometimes months if the family's wealthy: and trust me, they were wealthy. Festivities were still in full swing weeks later. To us, who had never attended a wedding outside the camp, the opulence was breathtaking. The bride looked beautiful, all dolled up and dripping with gold; the food tasted familiar but somehow elevated, even if just by the environment in which it was served. I ate foods I would never eat at home; everything tasted better in Kandahar.

As we got introduced, my sister was beside herself: finally, women worth her attention. They all looked so stylish, so fashionable. It is not the first thing I normally notice, but here, it was unmissable. According to my sister, they even had the latest style of eyebrow shaping, something out of the Bollywood movie that only came out the month before. I took her word for it.

My sister ruled the night: they all embraced her. I knew this trip was so far all about me: my tests; my desire to go back to Afghanistan. That night, I was quiet, determined to let her shine, keeping all my inappropriate thoughts to myself. Sangeena was taken by the beauty of the house, the beauty of our hosts. I just kept wondering how on earth they could afford all this.

My eyes were darting around, and I noticed a couple of girls sitting with their mother at the other side of the carpet. They looked out of place. Their clothes were clean but definitely not wedding-worthy, not even this late into festivities when things are a little more relaxed and you don't have to carry your weight in gold around your neck. They were too far from me to talk to them during dinner, but once we were done eating, I followed the mother into the kitchen. She politely inquired about my mother and asked me to send her regards. One of the girls walked in, her scarf around her head very tightly. She sat in the corner, away from us, positioning herself in front of the TV.

Emboldened by the fact that the mother obviously knew my

family, I peppered her with questions, establishing family back-ground and family lines, trying to figure out how exactly we were related. With our large families, every time you meet a new rel-ative, you treat them like a hostile witness: it is completely ap-propriate to engage in cross-examination. I wasn't out of line; it's practically expected.

Once the family connection was sufficiently mapped out, the mother explained that they came to this house only recently, when, as she put it, "their circumstances changed." She was related to my great-uncle through marriage. Her husband, my great-un-cle's son, was the second in command in the Afghan National Army. It takes far less than that to end up on the Taliban's hit list, so a bunch of Talibs stormed their home and murdered her husband, killing him in front of the children. After that, she said, she and the kids had nowhere to go, and they were taken in by my great-uncle.

Once she finished her story, she kept talking, pleasantly, dif-fusing the tension and the heaviness in the air that a story like that inevitably leaves behind, as if to ease my pain of having to hear it: "We are here now, and the children are getting better. It will be okay, Inshallah. It is nice to have a wedding in the house; it's such a happy occasion. It makes everybody cheerful."

She sounded almost apologetic for bringing up her own trag-edy. She clearly had to tell her story before and knew that those who heard it would find it difficult to continue with small talk, so she took it upon herself to overcome the silence. She talked about her kids and told me that the girls' names were Hasina and Husniya. As if on cue, Husniya, the girl that was until then sitting quietly in the corner, yelled out that the show was about to start. Hasina came running, sat down, and asked Husniya to turn the volume up. To my astonishment, she did so in Hindi.

I immediately switched my attention to the girls.

"I thought you've always lived in Kandahar. How on earth do you speak Hindi?" I eyed her suspiciously.

I spoke several languages, but I am a refugee and had to learn them to fit into all those colliding worlds. Why would this girl need to know Hindi?

"Everybody here speaks Hindi," she said, shrugging her shoulders. "It's the TV. You can't watch any of the shows if you don't speak Hindi, so you learn."

"We went to school before all this," Hasina added casually. "We only stopped after they killed my father. Our cousins took us in and it's only since then that we're not allowed to go to school anymore."

There was a storm of thoughts in my head, all of them simultaneously competing for my attention. The most persistent one, the loudest of them all was a realization that the girls were denied education in my own family. Here I am, calling out government officials and pointing fingers, sitting across the table from the girls who are denied that right by my own family members. Up until a minute ago, I thought of my great-uncle as nothing but a man kind enough to help out family by taking them in. Now I wasn't sure anymore. I didn't know what to think. He allowed the boys to continue with school, but the sisters, once equal, were now little more than the house servants. They were there to get the little boys dressed, to make sure the boys were clean and ready to go out into the world—the world they themselves didn't have access to anymore. The girls' days were now filled with embroidery, cleaning, and biding time until they got married.

I knew I couldn't throw a fit. I couldn't say a word. For all my lack of social graces, I knew that calling out my great-uncle would be beyond the pale, a mortal offense that not even my father could look past. You're meant to respect your elders no matter how misguided you may find their opinions.

I fancied myself this fearless advocate, and now that I'd met girls who needed help defending, I wasn't even speaking up. Sitting in that kitchen, I felt small, reminded of my limitations. There was a name for it, I realized. I was a hypocrite.

When we left their house that night, I struggled to fall asleep. I kept thinking about an argument I'd had with one of my uncles years ago. I must have been thirteen, and my father was, yet again, in prison—same old story: another one of our villagers went missing, my father asked too many questions, so he was locked up. This time they kept him there for a month. An uncle who had assumed my father's role as the head of the household was the one who objected the loudest to all the money that was spent on my education. He and his family emigrated to Canada years ago, but they kept visiting regularly. One evening after dinner, my uncle started berating me for attending the co-ed school. I don't know that I took it all that seriously: he did so immediately after he finished showing us slides from Canada, featuring all of his children, girls and boys, wearing shorts, happy and fully integrated into Canada's co-ed system. From there, he somehow seamlessly transitioned into saying that my co-ed school attendance was a source of family shame and that I needed to quit. I laughed at first, involuntarily, nervously, thinking it was just a bad joke. Once I realized he was serious, I wasn't entirely sure what to say, so for once I stayed quiet. I was hoping he would eventually realize he was being foolish and drop it. I just needed to sit it out. This was hardly the first time he'd spoken disparagingly about my education.

I was in the middle of the war with the Mean Girls of Quetta, and not entirely enamored with that school myself, but dropping out was not what I wanted to do. I thought I should say something, so I went to speak to my aunt, looking for advice. She's a teacher, after all; she seemed like a good person to ask.

Usually, me "saying something" is what my family had been

trying to prevent at all costs from the moment I first learned to talk, so I was shocked when my aunt agreed with me.

"Tell him that your education is your father's choice. If he wants to discuss it, he should discuss it with your father, not with you."

The next time my uncle brought up me quitting school, I repeated what my aunt told me, word for word.

"It's my father's decision, not mine. You should take it up with him."

My aunt was right; that ended the conversation.

The bitter aftertaste from that situation stayed with me for years, yet I don't think I quite understood the implications. It was only after meeting Husniya and Hasina that I fully grasped the precarious position I was in all those years ago. With my father in prison, my uncle was the head of the family. Had the Pakistanis decided to keep my father in prison longer, or not release him at all, as they sometimes did, my uncle would have been the one making the decision about my education, and I could have been the one denied school, watching Hindi series in someone else's kitchen as the highlight of my day.

This is not to say that I was completely unaware of the tensions within the family. As a child, my favorite Disney character was Simba, from *The Lion King*, with his mean uncles, and his fight for what's rightfully his. Obstinate from an early age, I'd make my entire family sit down with me and watch new episodes on Sahara TV every morning before school. They all had to cheer Simba on, and boo on cue as soon as Scar appeared. My mother remembers that I kept commenting on the family dynamics: apparently, I really didn't like Simba's uncle. The day after meeting Husniya and Hasina, my father, Sangeena, and I drove back to Quetta in silence. None of us had gotten much sleep the last few days. Sangeena, with her supernatural ability to sleep wherever you put her, dozed off as soon as we got in the car. But there would be no sleep for me. My mind was racing. I was finally given the last pieces of the puzzle, and it was time to put it together. I thought about the girls I'd met in Afghanistan, about the issues they faced. They seemed different on the surface, but there was a common thread: they all wanted to learn, but it was *going* to school that was the problem.

The entire modern history of Afghanistan can be seen as one long armed and violent argument about whether or not girls should be educated. One way or the other, all the upheavals, all the wars had something to do with educating us. It was Queen Soraya who started the fight for women's rights in the 1910s, at the same time as her contemporaries around the world. Afghan women were granted the right to vote in 1919, a year before the American women achieved theirs. It was Queen Soraya who opened the first all-girls school in Afghanistan. We were winning there for a bit. But as a result of power struggles and tribal disputes, as well as too much modernity too soon; Queen Soraya and the ruling family were exiled. Women's rights were exiled with them. It stayed that way until, in 1964, women were finally given equality in the constitution, and everybody was back in school. That happily-ever-after didn't last very long, either. The internal power struggle went on for years, until the Soviets decided to invade, and all of Afghanistan was united by the common enemy.

The Soviets were definitely girl-education friendly, possibly too friendly. With a decree, they turned all the schools co-ed, expecting Afghan boys and girls to show up the following morning in the same classroom. What they found instead were tribesmen up in arms. Men and women in our culture have separate lives; a decree from a foreign invader was not going to change that.

Conflict is inevitable when you don't bother to learn history before invading. As a result, all schooling stopped. There was no time to educate anyone now, especially not in the tribal areas, and our literacy rates plummeted to an all-time low. Those educated mostly fled, and the ones who were left behind were too busy trying to survive to worry about reading. Finally, some sort of equality was achieved—now everybody was illiterate.

After all that, the rise of the Taliban seemed almost inevitable: it was a self-fulfilling prophecy. They decided that what kept the country back was a struggle about girls' education, that's what cost us years of war—and, well, they weren't wrong about that. It was time to end it: girls, they decided, would be banned from going to school altogether.

After the Taliban was bombed out of power in 2001, we had a new government, a new constitution. Women were back. After years of not being allowed to leave their homes without being accompanied by a male relative, Afghan women in Kabul were suddenly heading ministries and representing districts. For many, the struggle to get educated was finally over.

The fighting sent Taliban running for the hills. But you see, that's the problem. Those hills are where I'm from, where my tribe is from. None of those splendid Kabul victories ever reached the girls there. Big international donors weren't investing in education in tribal areas; being an active war zone, there was no way to check on the progress. It was left to the government, which quickly realized what a lucrative opportunity building schools represented. Whatever educational grants there were, they were spent on infrastructure, building schools that the Taliban promptly blew up as soon as soon as they laid down the last brick. Sometimes, they didn't even need to bother to blow them up: a lot of areas were still active war zones, and few ventured out of their homes as it was, let alone sent their kids to school. Schools sat empty.

I already knew that education is too narrowly defined for Afghan purposes, even before I came to Afghanistan. But a single visit there showed me that the brick-and-mortar thing just wasn't going to work. Not anymore. Girls there needed an education system that could survive twists of fate, one that could survive the change in favorable circumstances; they needed education independent of the schools that kept getting blown up. It needed to be portable, so that they could take it with them wherever they went no matter what happened. Education had to remain steady as their luck ebbed and flowed. How do you safeguard education against fate?

That's when I began to think that technology could be the answer. Look at Husniya, learning to speak Hindi just by watching TV. Our commitment to a single approach to learning, the all-or-nothing attitude, is leaving too many behind. Our reality has changed, and education never caught up. Maybe the thing to do was to upgrade my father's stealth approach, come up with a 2.0 version of it. Bring the mountain to Mohammed yet again.

I kept going back to the idea of tablets. With Durdana and the Hindi-speaking sisters still fresh in my mind, I was certain that I was onto something. As vastly different as their circumstances were, tablets would solve both their problems. Tablets were portable enough for the girls to take with them wherever they went, no matter what happened.

It would take me three years to figure out how, and I lost faith many times along the way. Still, every time I faltered, I thought of the girls I'd met on that first trip to Kandahar. I was still committed to helping Durdana. For the next two years, I'd teach her and direct her studies from afar. My father was paying for her textbooks, and whatever books she couldn't get in Spin Boldak, her brother would get from Kandahar city. We all tried to help. Durdana would go on to make the most of it. After a couple of years, she covered all the high school material she needed to master. She revised her dream of becoming a doctor, but she still stuck to medicine. Eventually, we found a school for her in Kandahar city. She graduated in May of 2021, and she's a midwife now. She holds a pencil like a pro.

6

T WAS TIME TO LET MY PARENTS KNOW THAT I HAD decided not to go to Oxford.

Predictably, the announcement caused pandemonium, with my mother's voice ringing the loudest. The way that normally gentle woman screamed, "You will do what?" was one of the most horrifying moments in my life. I lived through bomb blasts and death threats, but nothing drained the life out of me the way her voice did that day. And I was yet to get to the worst part. I opened with not going to Oxford, but that was burying the headline. They were clearly aware of my obsession with girls' education, but until now they didn't quite understand that all that good work that I was planning to do would take place in Afghanistan.

"University education is still a must, of course," I added helpfully. "But I could get it in Kabul, at the American University instead of at Oxford. It would be quicker, I could skip the preparatory year and go directly to college." I wasn't officially admitted at the American University, but that was a formality. I knew I aced the test. I explained that while I studied there, I would intern at one of the hundreds of NGOs that Kabul was dotted with; learn the ropes, like an apprentice. No time would be wasted. I had it all figured out.

Once my mother regained her ability to speak, which took a while, she started listing all the different reasons why this was a spectacularly bad idea. In all fairness to her, most, if not all of them were good points. The one bandied around most frequently that day and forever more, was "You're throwing your life away," a statement she saw as containing a self-evident truth and which required no further explanation. It just needed to be repeated over and over until it sunk in, punctuated by her trying to hit me with a slipper.

Throwing. Your. Life. Away.

My mother, who rarely left her kitchen, was probably best positioned to see Oxford for what it was: a promise of an outside world, mine for the taking. It was an opportunity denied to so many Afghan women. It was inconceivable that I'd even think about walking away from it.

Another reason she gave for this being a terrible idea was: "'Kabul is a war zone." My mother took it upon herself to point out the obvious. She'd bring up every suicide bombing in Kabul, every shooting incident, every death she could think of. There was no shortage of incidents for her to draw on. I didn't know what I was getting myself into, she maintained. When I referred to Afghanistan as "home," she shrieked: "Home? You saw Afghanistan for the first time a month ago! You know nothing about the world! Nothing! This! This!" She kept gesturing to our living room. "This is your home!"

Other reasons she'd list were far more personal: "You'll spend a lifetime getting your heart broken with every girl they marry off at nine! Just like your father!"

Again, a valid point. Both my father and I were prone to depression. It's hard to tell, when you live in a refugee camp, what's situational and what you're born with, but watching the hardships of others certainly seemed to hit the two of us stronger. My mother loved how kind my father was and how deeply he cared about his community, but it was hard to miss how painful it was for him to care as much as he did.

She inevitably ended on a note of despair: "All this education was meant to make your life better! And you choose to make it worse!"

Over the next few weeks, every time she detected any uncertainty in my voice, my mother saw an opening: "Go to Oxford, finish the school there, and then take over from your aunt if you want to teach." A PPE degree from Oxford seemed like a bit of overkill for that particular position, but she wasn't going to let up. There was a compromise to be had, she was sure of it.

My father stayed mostly silent.

Having spent a year discussing nothing but Oxford at the dinner table, our conversations now switched to "my plans." They were less concrete than one would hope, considering what I was giving up.

I wanted to educate girls.

It would entail a novel, revolutionary approach.

I did not yet know what that approach was, or how I'd go about it.

My father said he trusted me. He didn't understand, but he trusted me.

My mother neither understood nor trusted.

In hindsight, having to listen to an opiniated, clueless sixteen-year-old's plans to save the world surely qualified my parents for sainthood. I made up for the lack of clarity in my plans with forcefulness in my voice. I was never soft-spoken, but silencing my own doubts in this particular instance required yelling.

Few of my grandiose ideas made sense once I said them out loud in our kitchen. The op-eds I wrote were about responsibility and duty, but they rarely ventured into concrete proposals. It was time to stop complaining and start doing. It was harder than I thought. Over and over, I kept going back to the idea of using technology as an educational aid. It was a nod to my beloved Encarta, a nod to the Hindi-speaking sisters and Durdana. I could see the potential despite my inability to fully address the obstacles.

I made the mistake of mentioning the tablets to my mother. Her immediate reaction was to point out that I was conditioning the education of those who couldn't afford a TV on a gadget that costs three times as much. In a country that, for the most part, has no internet. She kept mercilessly poking holes in my plan, hoping that once I realized the futility of it, I would let go.

My father decided to look past the apparent stupidity of the idea and talked instead about how impossible it all seemed when he decided to open the community school that no one really wanted, and that somehow, they still managed. Big ideas didn't scare him. He thought of them as puzzles, requiring nothing but persistence and patience.

"Keep thinking, you'll find the way."

I wasn't sure how. Each morning I would get up and my ideas seemed to me dumber and dumber. My plan seemed less and less realistic whenever I opened my mouth. And I opened it a lot.

In the end, my parents agreed that I could go to Kabul. My father, because he believed I would be able to figure it out. He had the endless supply of goodwill and faith. My mother, the queen of the long game, agreed because she thought that even spending a short time in Afghanistan would surely bring me to my senses and I could still end up, if not at Oxford, maybe at one of the Pakistani universities.

I believe everyone should have parents like mine: the one parent that trusts you blindly, and the one that challenges every word that comes out of your mouth. The first one gives you ideals and courage, but it's the second one that teaches you to sharpen your arguments. I know I don't say it enough, but I thank God for mine every day.

I GOT MY RESULTS FROM THE AMERICAN UNIVERSITY BY TEXT: I WAS the highest scoring on the tests (*told you so*, I thought to myself as I read it) and they were delighted to offer me a place there. There was a caveat, however. In all our conversations, not even my mother thought to bring that one up as a possibility. I would have to pay for the privilege to attend, as they were fresh out of scholarships that year. Tuition for a year was $25,000, and the first payment was due next month. I felt a sharp pain in my stomach as I read it. Tuition? Having won a scholarship for the preparatory school, the thought of having to pay for the university never really occurred to any of us. The amount, as outrageous as it was, didn't matter. Even if we could afford somehow to pay for university, I knew I couldn't ask for any more money from my parents. I wouldn't. Not after I turned down a scholarship.

It was over. The proverbial end of the road.

My bedroom was upstairs, and I ran down to find my parents, still with the cell phone in my hand. By the time I reached them,

I was half-blinded by tears. I can still remember exactly where my parents were sitting: my father was at the dinner table, my mother on the sofa, watching something on TV. Once I saw the two of them, tears turned into uncontrollable sobs.

My father was the one to see me first. I was crying too hard for them to make sense of what I was saying, but it was easy enough to guess that it was university related: we spent the whole year discussing nothing but that. I couldn't calm down enough to convey the message, so my father reached for my phone and read it.

"We'll get through it," he said immediately. He promptly launched into his childhood stories, his go-to preamble to any "we shall overcome" speech, recalling how poor he was when his mother left his father, how hopeless it all appeared for a while, how he walked barefoot for years, but it all changed. His stories rarely helped, but his voice never failed to soothe me.

And just as I was starting to calm down, he ruined it. He ended on "God will provide," which would have been words of comfort had my very pious mother said them. Coming from him, who was hardly religious at all, it sounded more like desperation.

It was my mother's turn to be silent. I knew her mind went to the same place all our minds went: the scholarship I so arrogantly declined. But she didn't bring it up. No one brought up how much money went into educating me. No one brought up sacrifices that we all had to make. They didn't bring up how difficult it was to fight with everybody in the family, all the time, about the path I was on. It was exhausting to defend their choices constantly. I knew that well. My going to Oxford was finally going to shut everybody up. It served as irrefutable evidence that my parents' choices were justified. Announcing my acceptance to the preparatory program was more than a source of pride, it was a long overdue relief. My mother was able to catch her breath, silence the cacophony of opinions about the futility of educating girls. When I declined, I took that away from them. And now, I wasn't going to university at all. Not going to Oxford was a blow, but not attending a university was a punch in the gut that left her breathless.

Yet they were still there, standing by me.

As an Afghan refugee in Pakistan, you grow up on a strange mix of cultures: Afghan tribal codes, mixed in with Bollywood and Hollywood, with a bit of BBC Pashto thrown in. To say that we're culturally confused is an understatement. Given that most of the people around me struggled to get any type of education, that the very concept of choice was unfamiliar, my situation required falling back on non-Afghan references.

If you follow American movies, which I do—religiously—it seems that the only time a Hollywood movie doesn't have a happy ending is when a kid drops out of school. Hollywood teaches you that it's possible to overcome childhood adversity, abuse, homelessness, that you can do anything—as long as you don't drop out of school. I found myself in the middle of a cautionary teen drama, a college dropout—before even starting the first class. Between my mother's voice and the plots of the teen movies I could now recall with eerie precision, I started to think there was no known trajectory but down.

On that note, effortlessly, like a child going down a slide, I slipped into depression.

There's not much to say about the next few months. I wish I could say I worked hard, but I didn't. There were no more forced family breakfast discussions about what I was going to do. For all the annoyance those meetings caused, my parents were far more alarmed now that they stopped. I deferred for a year, and I was going to keep deferring it until someone offered me a scholarship.

Which they may or may not do. Forging any different path eluded me. I was brought down by hubris.

It all seemed pointless: Who's going to listen to a high school graduate lecturing people? And about education of all things?

It was my father who refused to admit defeat. It was he who looked for an internship with an NGO for me now, determined to make me see that none of this is final, that nothing is fatal. A slight detour, he insisted, nothing else. The finish line never changed, and although I couldn't see it anymore, he tried to reassure me that it was still there. He stubbornly ignored my half-hearted objections and took over figuring out the practicalities of getting to it. While there was no university *for now*, his voice growing louder several decibels in emphasis, the internship plan was still achievable. That too was education, and I needed the knowledge of practical issues involved in running a nonprofit. I needed familiarity with daily requirements of that job. I could still concentrate on that while waiting for the scholarship committee to come up with money.

He made phone call after phone call, trying to find an NGO that would take me as an intern. I let him. Not out of conviction, but out of indifference. The world had ended as far as I was concerned and he was just sweeping the debris, trying to make the postapocalyptic landscape look prettier. He kept talking, I kept nodding.

He found an internship with an agricultural NGO dealing with one of Afghanistan's biggest exports: pine nuts. It was a far cry from what I wanted to do, but the NGO was properly run, and it wasn't corrupt—God only knows how he managed to find the one that wasn't. It was a good enough starting point.

I didn't quite perk up, but I did join his efforts and slowly started working toward it.

My mother was never very fond of the idea of me going to Kabul, even with the university education thrown in. But the suggestion of not going to university at all pushed her into a quiet despair. Nothing had really changed: my ideas were still vague, I was still young, and Kabul was still a war zone. Yet despite all of those concerns, she knew that not going to Kabul would be worse.

My parents were now united in the decision to make their eighteen-year-old daughter go on her own to Kabul to pursue her not-quite-yet-formulated dream. Even I was slowly getting excited about it all, a testament to my father's tenacity. I started getting ready to move to Kabul. I was filling up my green suitcase with all the things I imagined I would need there. I was smarter by then: I had my shalwar kameez, my Punjabi clothes, a set of loose pants and a long tunic, for the ride to the airport, but for when we got to Kandahar, I had a chador which covers you fully and doesn't make you stand out. Once in Kabul, I would revert to my Pakistani outfit. Getting across Afghanistan required a Beyoncé-like number of wardrobe changes.

My father walked in as I was putting my charger in my backpack. He was holding a white headscarf he got for me as a parting present. White headscarves are only worn by old women. Younger women choose color and patterns and embroidery, but I liked its simplicity. However, this scarf was too short.

"I'm a big girl! This scarf can't cover me!"

My father laughed. "You don't need a tent; it's just for your hair."

He explained that Khan Bibi used to wear white scarves like that.

"There is so much of her in you, you know. You love Afghanistan the way she loved it: not for the riches, not for the past, but for the possibilities."

He was right, of course. I was like a sports fan supporting a team that never stands a chance of winning, but who nevertheless goes into every game cheering it on.

After three generations, one of us was returning to Afghanistan to live there. To him, it was momentous.

It dawned on me that he was proud of me. I couldn't understand why, not after all this mess of my own making; but he was clearly proud of me. *I'm going to pick myself up, dust myself off, and give him an actual reason to feel that way*, I vowed.

I was flying out of Kandahar. It was the quickest and the cheapest way to get to Kabul from Quetta. My father would drive me across the border and to the airport. On our way there, he tried to squeeze in every last bit of guidance, a random collection of philosophical thought and practical advice:

"If somebody is trying to harass you, or a group you are in, slap his face in front of everyone. Let it be his shame. That way, he will never do it to another woman."

"Always take a stand. If you believe in something it's worth fighting for it."

He then immediately added, "You should be a winner, not a martyr in pursuit. Martyrdom doesn't mean anything at the end of the day if you are not there to see the end of the fight."

Put together, it amounted to "fight, but know when to stop." He had a feeling that latter would become a source of struggle, knowing that recognizing when to stop was never my strong suit.

I listened as intently as I did when I was a child sitting at his feet after he came back from the dead. Only this time, it was a reminder of my mortality that prompted the conversation, not his. I was the one going off to war.

It was uncomfortable for both of us, this flood of emotions. Neither one of us knew how to deal with it, how to behave. Few would accuse Pashtuns of being in touch with their feelings, and on several occasions my father looked like he'd rather shoot his way out of this conversation than continue talking.

He stuck with it though.

If he worried about my depression, he didn't say anything. He was sending me off with love, keeping his fears to himself.

He talked all the way to the airport. When they called my flight, I reached for his hand and kissed it, as is the custom, to show my love and respect, and to say goodbye.

In response, he put his hand on my head, to bless me. We stood there, neither of us knowing what to say, finally out of words. And then, almost as an afterthought, he pulled me toward him and wrapped his arms around me, the way he used to when I was a child. Both shocked by this sudden display of emotion, we muttered our goodbyes and I walked away to the gate. I didn't look back because it would have taken only one look at my father for me to change my mind and stay.

7

KABUL WASN'T THE HOMECOMING I'D IMAGINED; it offered none of the peace I felt in Kandahar. The place had all the unease and discomfort of walking in a pair of shoes several sizes too small.

I soon learned that my Dari, the language of choice in Kabul, had a long way to go. An occasional slip into Pashto had people frowning with contempt for yet another tribal newcomer to the city, but it was my Urdu accent that made everyone suspicious: obviously, I must be a Pakistani spy.

If fitting in as a refugee into Pakistani society seemed hard, fitting in in Kabul as a returning one seemed practically impossible. Kabul liked nothing about me. It did not like my accent, did not like my clothes, and it most definitely did not like my ideas.

I disliked it right back. I winced every time I saw those newly built palaces dotting Kabul like someone had randomly placed cupcakes along the city grid. They belonged to the new elite: politicians and warlords. The two categories often overlapped. Their mansions were painted in colors that made them resemble a dessert buffet at a wedding. The architecture had little to do with our culture, with our history. *This is nothing like Kandahar*, I couldn't help thinking.

The pervasive sense of uncertainty that Kabul exuded made me mildly paranoid—probably for a good reason. Within days of me arriving, I witnessed my first attack.

I was at my cousins', crying to my mom on the phone over something trivial—a shopkeeper being rude or something equally dumb—when I heard an explosion. I ran to the window. It is the very last thing you should do when you hear a blast, but I'd never heard an explosion before and had no idea what to do. I often wondered how come we weren't born knowing that you're meant to run away from the loud boom, not toward it? Shouldn't that be instinctive?

Through the window I saw a whirl of dust and smoke, and a man's shoulder suspended on the electricity lines above the explosion site. When the smoke cleared, I could see what was once a white van that carried people around town. It was now just twisted metal and broken glass. There was blood and flesh everywhere. I hung up on my mother, not knowing how to explain what just happened. She kept trying to call back, probably panicked, but I just let it ring and ring in my hand.

My cousins ran in to see what happened, promptly bursting into tears at the sight, inconsolable.

Although I was in tears before the bomb went off, I noticed

my cheeks were dry now. I didn't feel the need to react at all. I just stood there, paralyzed. Even crying required too much effort.

There is no prescribed, universally appropriate reaction to a bombing. Being a woman, however, both crying and keeping your composure seemed somehow to be wrong choices. If you cry, you're immediately dismissed as weak. If you don't, you're considered heartless.

I decided it was preferable not to cry. Preconditioned by all those years of having to prove I was no weaker than the boys, I would always err on the side of strength. It would take me years to understand that crying had nothing to do with strength. Crying is necessary. Crying is what makes you different from the dead.

My mother was right, I knew nothing of living in a war zone. You imagine epic courage and heroic efforts, when in reality it's only random deaths around you. It's fear and confusion and images that are burned into your retinas until it makes you want to scratch your eyes out.

The year I chose to come to Kabul was the year of unprecedented violence, a beginning of an end, although we didn't know it yet. Soon, I felt numb to all the dying around me. Afghan Kochi women, who get tattoos as a part of their culture, have a saying: "If you hit one spot more than forty times with a needle, you become numb, and the spot becomes blue."

That's what Kabul did to me: it made me numb and blue.

I threw myself into work. In those rare spare moments when I wasn't doing spreadsheets on Afghanistan's pine nut production or trying to figure out how to educate women in rural areas, I was running my mouth. It didn't take long before I switched from writing op-eds about the faults of the Pakistani government to writing about the faults of the Afghan one. I like to make friends everywhere I go. I was criticizing the Taliban for the violence and the government for their impotence to prevent it. They were the two sides of the same coin, I insisted. The government was no more than the white-collar version of the Taliban, ruthlessly pillaging their people, their own country, their own culture. Within the first couple of months of my coming back to Afghanistan, I managed to offend anyone who mattered.

By now, I had some political credentials, and it wasn't just security services looking for dissenters who followed me. I was invited to speak at the Pashtun Tahafuz Movement (PTM) conference. This group gathered every year, and they wanted me to be the keynote speaker. I was going to be the first woman to address the conference, and the first one ever to do so in Pashto. Cultural significance aside, it was probably a good thing, given the state of my Dari.

The program that was distributed at the conference listed me as speaking first. There was a professor who was scheduled to speak immediately after me and I took exception to the order of speeches. He was much older than me, far more respected; I insisted he should go first. My parents would never forgive me if I went before him; they were still shouting instructions about propriety in my mind. "Please, sir. I will go after you." He accepted, graciously, and I walked back to my seat in the first row to wait my turn.

It couldn't have been more than a couple of minutes into his remarks when an explosion ripped through the tent. The last thing I heard before the blast was my name, the professor was thanking me. The force of the blast sent me flying, and when I landed, I couldn't hear anything. It was not deafness caused by the absence of sound, but by an overabundance of it: your hearing is gone until the buzzing stops echoing, until you can again distinguish between those lesser sounds—screams, commotion, the sound of feet running.

I slowly took in what was happening. The professor was lying on the stage, bleeding profusely. So was Zahed, the cameraman who was standing in front of me. He was blocking my view just a minute ago. Zahed was the one closest to the bomb. When the bomb went off, he blocked more than my view. His body blocked the debris from reaching me. I owed him my life.

The whole tent was filled with hundreds of people who all knew what to do. I, apparently, didn't.

I witnessed shootings in our home, but I'd never been in a public place for something like this. At home, if there was gunfire, you were meant to run toward the injured people and try to get them to safety. That's our tribal code, the one that had been drummed into me, and the one that I instinctively followed.

But this wasn't a shooting, and this wasn't family.

Immediately after the explosion, before I even properly came to, the girls around me started pushing me toward the exit, trying to get me out of there, saying that we were the target. Their words didn't quite register. My main concern was Zahed. He was injured, and I wasn't going anywhere without him. I tried to get to him, pushing against the tide of people running toward the exit.

The girls kept trying to redirect me, thinking I was confused, unsure of the direction in which I was supposed to run. Eventually, the men joined in, helping to drag me out. I kept yelling, saying they should carry out the injured, that they should help Zahed. I don't know if whatever was coming out of my mouth was making sense, or even whether they could hear me at all in that mayhem, but my yelling was ignored, and the struggle continued. I was now crawling back, headscarf still hanging loose from the blast.

When I finally managed to get to Zahed, I clutched him, refusing to let go. Eventually, the men around me realized that we were a package deal and helped me carry him out.

Outside, the gunfire was everywhere. It's how the Taliban works. The first blast is normally just the beginning. They either detonate a second bomb that goes off as people start running out, or you find them perched on the roofs of neighboring buildings, taking people out one by one. This time around it was the latter. Of course, a PTM conference meant everyone in the tent was a known activist and therefore everyone was a target.

The gunfire sent everyone running, and I was once again left to drag Zahed out to safety by myself. I was covered in blood, unable to tell which one of us was bleeding. I kept pushing and dragging and then pushing again until I got him to my friend's car.

My friend drove us to the hospital. I sat in the back seat holding Zahed's head, watching the life slowly drain out of him. The drive seemed interminable, with Kabul traffic barely moving as Zahed's blood kept soaking the seats.

When we finally got to the hospital, the entire building was surrounded by special forces: the president was visiting the hospital. They weren't allowing the cars in, so I got out of the car to explain that we had a man in the back seat who was about to bleed out.

"You need to let us in."

They refused. They said there was a security protocol in place, and they weren't supposed to allow anyone in. I argued, pleaded, begged. "What kind of security protocol keeps the dying away from the hospital?" I cried out in desperation. They were unmoved. Having run out of arguments, I just kept repeating, "He was so young, he was so young," already a lament, already in past tense, like a future foretold.

It was my fault, I suddenly thought, I'm the reason he's bleeding out.

I felt the weight of all my decisions: it was my fight, my beliefs, yet he's the one who was dying in the back seat of the car. The bomb wasn't meant for him. I didn't quite dare to finish that thought, not yet.

It became clear that no amount of begging was going to make the soldiers change their minds, and so I turned around. By the time I got back to the car, Zahed was dead. He had bled out, lying in an improbably large pool of blood. He died alone while I was arguing with the soldiers. His eyes were still open. I wondered what it was that he looked at last.

Now that he was dead, the hospital authorities were happy to accept him. They didn't want him alive, but the dead apparently weren't a threat to protocol. We were told to wait outside, and we did, not sure what was supposed to happen next. I wasn't even prepared for the logistics of dying.

We stayed outside the hospital the entire afternoon and then into the night, trying to estimate how many people were injured and who was being brought in.

Once I got home, I called my father. Before I even had a chance to explain to him what happened, he scolded me for going to a place that is an obvious target. At some point, standing outside that hospital, the words that everybody kept repeating sunk in: it was quite possible that we were the target. The bomb was supposed to go off during my speech. My father clearly didn't know it yet, and I wasn't going to make matters worse by clarifying.

I summoned up the last bit of rebellion inside me, fueled by the adrenaline still pumping through my body, and I pointed out to my father that it was he who had taught me to stand up for things, and it was a little late for the course correction. "It's who I am. It's how you brought me up. You can't change your mind now."

He didn't get a chance to respond because he was interrupted by my mother screaming in the background, tired of heroism, tired of losses, telling me to come home, that she'd had enough. I could tell my father was trying to cover the phone so I wouldn't hear her yelling, but it made little difference. I heard her words and I steeled myself to explain the other thing which was sure to reach him eventually: that I dragged a man out, that I'm not entirely sure if my hair remained covered or whether my top rolled up when I was crawling and worse, that the general consensus was that I clearly didn't care.

But parda, our strict code of separation of men and women, would surely fade into insignificance compared to a loss of life? "They can't hold it against me, right?"

My father was less certain. "You have to be careful, child," he said. "Afghans don't forgive their women lightly. You cannot ignore the rules." His tone didn't match his words, however: there was pride in his voice. With or without a headscarf, I did the right thing. I didn't fail him.

When I hung up, I realized I was still covered in blood. It was everywhere—on my skin, on my clothes. I went to wash it off. I kept scrubbing long after the blood was gone, I kept scrubbing for days.

As the adrenaline wore off, it felt like a slow fall into the abyss. The shock left my mind pitch-dark and thought-free. It would take days to wake up from that stupor.

Clinical, ugly, debilitating depression settled in. The kind where you cannot get up, where you don't feel like you can keep going, and even opening your eyes presents an unsurmountable effort. It's a cocoon of darkness lit up only by the incessant, involuntary memory flashes of horror that landed you there in the first place.

Short sequences involving explosions and running.

Details like the ringing in the ears, or Zahed's dead eyes, would catch up with me out of nowhere and I'd be unable to shake them off.

Anything could send me there: the slamming of a door two

floors below me, or noise from the street coming through the window. There was no place to hide from it.

I'd come up for air only to wonder what I was doing in Afghanistan in the first place. It wasn't just the explosion, or the idea of being targeted. It was deeper than that. It was hearing over and over how inappropriately I behaved: "A woman! Dragging a man out!"

I wasn't necessarily hoping for pity, but some empathy would have been nice. There was none of it. My extended family was positively glowing with rage. Phone call after phone call, I had to listen to their outrage, knowing that they called my parents first, knowing that everything they were saying to me now, they'd already said to my parents. "You always think you know best, don't you?"

I committed that ultimate Afghan offense of publicly reaching for a man that was neither a relative nor a spouse. The least I could do was show some respect and listen to how much shame I had supposedly brought to my family.

I agonized over their reaction, their judgment. I couldn't comprehend that a man died and the only takeaway was that I shouldn't have tried to help because he was a man. It was a thought on a loop, unanswerable, ebbing and flowing through my mind.

I knew I couldn't wait out my depression, that I had to at least try to get going. Little by little, I started dealing with practicalities. I went back to work. I continued attending protests, which by August took over the entire country. We didn't really have a set of demands; we just wanted the killings to stop. It was not a movement, it was a desperation-propelled landslide, sending us downhill. Protests were just a noise we made on our way down.

There were plenty of things to protest against: Taliban bombs, drone attacks, and the government's indifference to it all. Although our rage was directed as much at the impotence of the government as the Taliban attacks, the government practiced selective hearing. From the social media storm that ensued, they would cherry-pick messages condemning the Taliban and retweet them. My tweets were particularly popular with the government. They were more than happy to amplify a rare tribal voice raging against the Taliban. They'd quickly scrolled through my other, less convenient tweets, criticizing *them*.

I started receiving death threats, which I mainly ignored. Not an act of bravery as much as a sign of resignation: I picked up on the Taliban's general displeasure with me the first time they tried to blow me up. If they're going to kill me, I might as well go on raging.

Even those around me who shared my desire for change, who protested with me, questioned whether it was worth continuing the fight quite so openly. They said I was taunting the Taliban. "Don't be stupid. Next time they won't miss."

I thought of my father's warning, the words he'd said before I came to Afghanistan: "Don't be a martyr in pursuit." I had no intention of being one. I didn't want to die. Of course I didn't want to die. But it is so easy to get lost, so easy to get swept up in it all. We talk about lines we shouldn't cross, but knowing when to stop is more like feeling your way out of the labyrinth blindfolded. You're stepping into a vortex; all control is lost.

When threatening me directly didn't yield desired results, the Taliban started calling my father. The callers offered detailed descriptions of my death—imminent, as they kept promising, unless I stopped protesting and writing. Above all, "No more tweets!" Threats were difficult enough for him to hear, but then he'd receive a slew of well-meaning phone calls. "Taliban is after Pashtana, she has to stop. They'll kill her." Somehow my father found those friendly warnings even worse. The callers assumed that we simply weren't aware of the threats, otherwise I surely would have stopped. That's when my father had to explain that I knew. That he knew.

A dozen or so friendly warnings later, my father called me. "This has to stop. Your mother is slowly but surely losing her mind." He paused for what seemed like an eternity, weighing his words. When he finally spoke, it wasn't what I expected to hear. "Please, just stop telling people whose daughter you are. Maybe then, they'll stop calling the house."

But the Taliban weren't the only ones paying attention to me. I got an invitation from Amnesty International to attend a seminar on freedom of expression. Finally, I thought, someone who appreciates a loudmouth. The seminar was taking place in Beirut. It was my first international conference and my first trip out of the country. I got my Afghan passport, which I relentlessly kept posting on social media, proud of it to no end. With a layover in Dubai, my trip technically counted as visiting two countries. I fancied myself a seasoned world traveler now.

I sent my mother a picture from my layover in Dubai—me, in my kamarchin. I couldn't believe my parents had allowed me to travel internationally on my own. My mother, whose international travel consisted of exchanging her Pakistani kitchen for the Afghan one, sent back encouraging-sounding comments that half-hinted at her *possibly* being proud of me. It made me smile. It didn't require much effort on my part to make my father feel proud, but my mother, no less loving, set her bar far higher. With her, words of praise were few and far between.

Beirut was just a momentary escape, but it was an exceptionally well-timed one. It was a different world. Lebanon was hardly problem free, but the country was decomposing in style. Everything looked different. People looked different. Buildings looked different. As I walked down Hamra Street, I saw so many students just hanging out. There was so much life. I kept thinking, *Just imagine if we had this in Kandahar.*

Attending the seminar was even more thrilling. I was surrounded by like-minded people. Not one of them wanted to blow me up. I was finally able to exhale. Morning sessions were mostly lectures, dealing with everything from the history of the idea of freedom of expression to its practical applications. By noon, my hand would hurt from all the note taking.

In the afternoon, we'd discuss what we'd learned that day. The very last day, they made me Amnesty's Global Youth Ambassador. It's still one of my proudest achievements.

As soon as I got back to Kabul, I called my parents. It was one of those epically long phone calls, with me recounting every detail of my trip. I never quite mastered editing my thoughts, not for content and definitely not for time. The two of them were an attentive and eager audience, wanting to hear it all, point by point. It sounded as if they really did want to know all about the shape of the soap in my hotel room.

It was going swimmingly, until my father let it slip, "I need to go now and deal with the funerals." I could hear my mother gasp as he said it. It was a difficult year, and we hardly had any happy conversations lately. Whatever joy we shared reliving my adventure quickly faded away.

My father tried to change the subject, but it was too late. I kept pressing until he finally told me what happened while I was away. The mood dampened immediately. Members of my extended family were killed in a drone attack in Kandahar Province on their way to a wedding. Seven women and nine children, all decked out and armed with henna for bridal tattoos, were packed up in couple of black Toyota Hiluxes to get to the bridal shower in a neighboring village. On their way back, the drone obliterated them.

Except for the drivers, there were no men in the cars; it was

only women and children. Two of the women were married to offi-
cers in the Afghan army fighting *against* the Taliban. You couldn't
get it more wrong if you tried. But I suppose we all look like the
Taliban from ten thousand feet.

In Islam, performing the last rites starts with washing of the
body, but there wasn't enough left of them for that. They were
robbed of everything, denied a proof of ever having existed.

My Beirut bliss was gone in an instant. Tired, I started search-
ing for information about the attack, but all I could find was a
short obituary on Facebook. No one was talking about it. My
anger slowly started building up. I started posting on my social
media, demanding that the government at least mention their
deaths. Our own provincial governor wouldn't say a word. No one
reposted my tweets, either. All I got was a privately posted message
from one of the politicians, expressing sympathy for my loss. "It's
regrettable, but we need to concentrate on who the enemy is." Her
approach confused me. Am I expected to pretend they just didn't
die? Do we just ignore the fact because it wasn't done by the "real
enemy"?

"A tragic mistake," she admitted, "but these things happen. It's
hardly news."

This was the proverbial straw that broke the camel's back.
"Tribal deaths are never news. When was the last time someone in
Kabul was killed by a drone attack? I bet everybody would be up
in arms then. This has nothing to do with the drones. Could it be
that you don't actually care about *us* dying? That you think we're
expendable?"

I kept typing and typing, long after she stopped responding.

I was tired of the government silence on tribal deaths in drone
attacks. They kept quiet to preserve the flow of money, not to con-
fuse the donors. I could accept that the deaths of those women and
children were a mistake, but the expectation that they shouldn't

be mourned, or their deaths mentioned, that they should be just written out due to inconvenience—that was unfathomable. They shouldn't be brushed under the rug like dirt, no matter how complicated it may be for the world to understand.

You don't make history simpler by ignoring parts of the population who don't fit into the narrative.

But here, even if the bombs don't get you, the oversimplification will.

8

SINCE GETTING CAUGHT UP IN THE BLAST, I WAS in constant physical pain. Even before the bombing, I was physically fragile. A few months prior to coming to Afghanistan, I had gotten into a car crash in Quetta. The doctor said I was lucky. My injuries were extensive but not too serious and I was going to heal in time. "You just need to be careful."

Getting blown up in Kabul some five months later didn't qualify as being careful. When the force of the blast sent me flying, I landed on the side I had already injured in the car crash. Old and new scars intertwined, going from my hand all the way to my neck, refusing to heal, as if my body if not my country had a finite capacity for violence.

My back pain was becoming unbearable. Your posture is always relative to your worries and fears, and for months, there was nothing to straighten my back. It was a vicious cycle. The stress kept me hunched, crumpling me like a piece of paper that's about to be discarded. That in turn made my physical injuries worse, which then added to my stress.

In time, the violence just integrated into our daily lives. No one was protesting anymore. We weren't at war exactly; we were just prey during open season. The Taliban's approach favored quantity over quality, knowing that wearing down our resistance didn't require precision of aim on their part. I think it is the randomness of it all that eventually gets you. Knowing that you're a target can strangely steel you, give you a sense of purpose, even if it is an illusion. Randomness just does your head in. Whatever reasonable precautions you may take, there's no guarantee that you won't find yourself in the wrong place at the wrong time. It's always hanging over your head.

The blast also added a hairline fracture to my cheekbone. I developed migraines, the world-stopping, debilitating kind. I tried to ease them with painkillers, but painkillers made me feel dizzy. Pain seemed preferable to bumbling around, so I stopped taking them altogether. I had no strategy to get better other than waiting it all out: the pain, the mayhem, the violence.

I'd explain my gloom away as PTSD. I knew that wasn't what it was. PTSD can only happen once the horrors stop. Here, trauma was never-ending, it just shape-shifted. We started measuring time and space in suicide bombings, using them as references and landmarks. After a while, when I heard explosions at night, I'd get up, make sure it's not my dormitory being attacked, and then go straight back to sleep, consoled by the fact that, if nothing else, today was not my turn. People can get used to anything. Even when the Taliban attacked the parliament, and then fought for it for days, I slept right through it.

Immediately after the blast, it didn't occur to me to go to the hospital to get checked out. No one wants to seek medical help for minor injuries when so many people around you are dying. It's embarrassing. There was a girl I knew who jumped out the window during the attack on Kabul University and broke her pelvis. Too poor to get an operation, she was left like that, with a broken pelvis, for forty days, until enough money was collected to get her admitted to a hospital. What right did I have to complain about some back pain?

By the time pain wore me down sufficiently to seek medical attention, there was little doctors could do about it. The nerves around my spine were irreparably damaged. Over the years, they would operate, but only in the hope of preventing it from getting worse. I hunched for too long.

I became an expert at ignoring the chaos around me and concentrated on work instead. I wasn't any closer to figuring out my lofty goal of bringing education to rural areas. Two paths persisted, not quite unified yet. One was the idea of tablets, which I refused to let go of, like a dog with a bone. The second one was setting up community schools. The only point of absolute certainty in my plan was the location: I wanted to work in rural areas. It seemed an obvious choice. Not only were rural areas the most vulnerable, but few of the educational programs ever managed to reach them. The farther you ventured from Kabul, the worse it got; the government spring cleaning consisted only of polishing objects sitting on bottom shelves, ignoring anything out of reach. The new and shiny Kabul stood in stark contrast with the rest of the country.

The majority of the tribal areas were not under government control, at least not fully, and even those that the government claimed to control were at best contested. Some were outright war zones, outside the reach of both the government and the NGOs.

Spin Boldak is the district where we became internally displaced people. Although it was nominally controlled by the government, the Taliban roamed freely and operated in parallel for years. Because of the proximity to the Pakistani border, it was a lucrative place to hold. There was money to be made on taxing the goods that left the country, legally or otherwise.

Kandahar Province overall didn't score high on the amenities list, but Maruf was abysmal even by Kandahar's standards. It stood as a shining example of the corruption that broke Afghanistan. Maruf had the lowest literacy rates and less infrastructure than any other district in the province. At the time, there were forty-two buildings allocated as schools, but only one of them was functioning. It was a game of whack-a-mole: the government would build the schools, then the Taliban would raze them to the ground. Those few that remained standing stayed intact solely because they were never used as schools. Their saving grace was that people forgot why they were built in the first place.

In the entire district, there was a single school serving seventy-two villages that were miles and miles apart, crisscrossed by frontlines. Because of that one school, that one building functioning as it was intended, the government claimed that schooling was available in the entire district. Low literacy rates were blamed on the villagers not allowing their children to attend. Details like distances and frontlines that prevented people from sending their children there were left out of the government reports. It made it easier for government to convince the donors that, despite their best efforts, it was a tribal, cultural thing that prevented any progress.

For two decades, stubbornly and without anything to show for it, the government kept pouring education money into brick and mortar. They built an entire shadow economy around schools that existed only in government expenditure, never in reality. They'd pay yearly salaries to teachers who never taught a day in their life. They'd encourage donors to send books that would inevitably end up being used as kindling in the winter. In fully illiterate households there was no other purpose for them.

Decisions about rural areas were made within the gray walls of government buildings, miles away, and the two worlds didn't coincide at all. There was the chaotic world we inhabited, and the bureaucratic one, the one with degrees and infrastructure—orderly, planned, and organized alphabetically.

I came to know Spin Boldak well. On my way to visit my parents, I would always take the same route: I'd fly to Kandahar and then someone from the tribe would drive me across the border into Quetta. I'd stop in Spin Boldak because of Durdana. Every time I was there, I'd get angrier and angrier. There was still no public school there. Spin Boldak, I'd decided, was where I should start.

Interestingly, there was one school for girls in Spin Boldak, the one that students attended in reality and not just on paper, but the government had nothing to do with it. It was an underground school for the internally displaced people (IDPs). IDPs from the Farah Province started the whole underground schooling adventure during the Taliban, in the '90s, like my father did. They had their own community schools, hosted in private homes, that followed the government curriculum. The downside was that the schools were far from Durdana's village so she couldn't just walk there. The IDPs were here temporarily, and so was their school, even if occasionally "temporary" turned out to last decades. Community school education was a concept that traveled well, and it was easily replicated wherever they ended up settling. Given that millions of Afghans kept moving around like a traveling circus, it was immensely useful as a template.

I wanted a 2.0 version of that system, with one major difference: I wanted it out in the open. I had enough of education being treated like some shameful secret. I wanted the blessing of both the government and the tribal community. "My NGO"—for there was going to be an NGO, I never doubted that—"will offer education that wouldn't have to hide." I was done being underground.

By far the biggest obstacle was the lack of available teachers, especially female teachers. There were plenty of girls wanting to be educated, but no one to teach them. It was a tale of unrequited love: being denied access to schools for so long, degrees were few and far between in the district. To make it work, I needed to find women who were educated within their own homes, informally. All around Afghanistan, you can still find families that we call "well-read," those who schooled their own children, when all access to schools was barred, holding on to their bookshelves from one generation to another. It was the kind of homeschooling that, outside of Afghanistan, only existed in eighteenth-century English novels. In twenty-first-century Afghanistan, these families became the perfect pool from which to recruit my teachers.

The search for teachers took months, until finally a friend of mine said his sisters, Zarghona and Nazo, would be interested. They turned out to be some distant relatives. These sisters could not have been more different. Zarghona was full of life, loud, and once she started teaching, she'd put the fear of God into children with a force and ferocity I hadn't seen since I watched my aunt in action. Nazo, on the other hand, was empathy personified: soft-spoken and patient. I had no viable reference for her, because I hadn't come across anyone as soft-spoken and patient as she is.

I offered them a stipend, out of pocket—my father's pocket at first—not quite amounting to a salary. Although I wasn't taking money from my parents for myself, asking my father to pay *them* qualified as a tribal expense. I insisted, quite forcefully, that teaching should be a paid position, community school or not. I wanted it to be perceived as employment, not just by the women, but also the tribe.

Nazo shrugged her shoulders when I mentioned the money, but Zarghona promptly tried to negotiate. "There's a designer headscarf I've seen, but you can only get it in Pakistan."

Apparently, she had been eyeing that scarf for months. "I don't really want the money; I want you to get me a headscarf from Quetta instead."

Eyeing the clothes I was wearing with a devastating combination of pity and disdain, she corrected herself: "Maybe you could ask your sister to get it for me. She'll know what to get."

I tried and failed to explain that exchanging her services for a headscarf defeated the purpose. "You're supposed to be paid for your services. It's how employment works." She was having none of it. In the end, we settled on her getting both the money and the headscarf, with me negotiating against myself and absorbing insults in the process. It was not an employers' market.

I still wasn't entirely certain how to get it all going. I talked to my father about it almost daily. If anyone knew about starting community schools, it was him. Although this was a different time, with different challenges than the ones he faced in the '90s, some things still applied. "Listen before you talk," he kept repeating over and over. "They know what they need. You just have to respond to the needs of the community."

Like a traveling salesman, I'd take a slight detour on my way to visit my parents, to talk to people, to figure out what was needed, how to best approach it. It was cheaper and quicker to fly to Kandahar from Kabul and then get a lift to Quetta than to fly directly. Driving through the province gave me plenty of opportunity to talk to people from my tribe. The list of needs was endless, but I kept writing them down. I would use this list to develop a curriculum, and whatever I couldn't fit into the curriculum, I'd label "a community project."

I pored over printouts of Indian curriculums. It seemed like a good template for what I was trying to do. But even as I got closer to finalizing content development, the delivery remained a problem.

I went to online schools looking for help; I spoke to people running Khan Academy, EdX, and Coursera. They were all pleasant enough, especially considering that they were talking to a teen in Afghanistan working off an impossible premise of establishing an online school in a country without the internet. However, they were of no help. In a world driven and defined by the connectedness, we Afghans sat there fragmented and divided, speechless. Everything I tried to do came with its own set of prerequisites, ranging from access to the internet to peace on earth.

I was weighed down by the crushing need to prove myself, for my sake, for my father's sake, for my family's sake. The whispers that were momentarily silenced with Oxford were now growing louder within my extended family. Not only was I not helping girls' education, which was bad enough in itself, I was starting to serve as an example to the contrary: "Look at all that money wasted on her education, for nothing. Eh, what do you expect when you start educating girls?"

I couldn't even pretend to ignore the dissenting voices; the guilt was crippling. The decision to educate me was now seen as an error in judgment. My father's judgment. After everything he'd done as a leader of our community, everything he'd done for me, I was now eroding his standing. My uncles made sure of it.

My mother called one day out of the blue. When I answered the phone, she was already screaming. Her call was clearly a sequel to a conversation she had had with someone else, although I never learned which particular uncle got her into a frenzy.

"Do you know what your father has to go through to defend you? Do you understand the rift this is causing in the family?" The questions were clearly rhetorical; she never paused long enough to give me an opportunity to respond. Then came the nail in the coffin: "Do you know how much pain your father's in?"

In the background, I could hear my father's valiant, if useless, efforts to stop her. "Don't tell her that. Stop saying that." But we all knew my mother was right. I was becoming a stain on his reputation. That's what hurt the most. I thought self-sufficiency would be enough to keep the rest of the family quiet. It wasn't.

I needed a victory, not a tie.

The one good thing that came from me returning to Afghanistan was that it led my parents and siblings to start cautiously spending time in Kandahar. It felt as if my return broke the curse. They weren't ready to permanently move back—those who had a choice, chastened by history, always kept their feet firmly planted in other countries. Still, there was now a house in Kandahar that I could call home. I imagined that one day, maybe, I'd become a part of our family's folklore, like Khan Bibi, but in reverse: I'd be the woman that led us back.

But there was a far more obvious point of comparison between us two. For both my grandmother and me, crossing the Durand line was a fall from grace. Like her, once across, I was broke. Completely, tragically broke. I went from attending top private schools in Pakistan to chewing stale bread in my Kabul dorm room to ward off hunger so I could fall asleep. I made daily choices between eating or content development, and proper meals too often slipped down the ladder of importance. I tried to take additional paying jobs, but between setting up the NGO and interning at one, there were not enough hours in the day that would allow for a job that would make a serious difference in my finances.

I must have sent a thousand emails to various NGOs, trying to get funding, but I suspect most of them simply stopped reading as soon as they saw the words "digital learning." I never heard back from any of them. It all came back to the issue of connectivity; I needed to figure out how to make digital learning work without an internet connection.

With my usual grace, I stumbled upon a solution in the form of a casual, private message on Facebook from a friend, unaware that he was about to change my life: "Hey, did you hear that there's an NGO that preloads educational content on tablets?" and then he forwarded an article. The article was about Rumie, a Canadian NGO that supports education in ways and places that few can—or bother to—reach.

That was it, Rumie was my prince in shining digital armor. Their preloaded, solar-powered tablets were the answer to my prayers. Costing about fifty bucks each, less than a tenth of the cost of the regular tablet, they were affordable, they were easy to use, and they didn't require the internet. They ticked every single box. Everything about them was suitable. They were even made of plastic. Good luck putting those in the fire when it gets cold, the way people did with books.

I reached out to Rumie, and we hit it off immediately. Rumie is one of those rare organizations that seemed unaware of the existence of a box that one is supposed to be thinking in. They had a penchant for unconventional ideas, and as my idea was borderline crazy, it definitely qualified.

Rumie generously agreed to give me five pre-loaded tablets so I could pilot the program. I had people in place, ready to go. I was armed with both the content and a way to deliver it. At long last, I had a workable plan.

It was time to get the government's blessing.

I lost count of how many ministries I had to go to. The touring of all those government offices killed my will to live. I was too broke to pay for the full taxi ride, so I'd ask the cab driver to take me as close to wherever I was going that day as my money would allow. Sometimes it was a twenty-minute walk to get to where I needed to be, but often it would take an hour. I'd inevitably arrive exhausted and frustrated. The heavily policed areas, barricades, and checkpoints rendered any direct route impossible. I'd feel uneasy walking up to ministries; they were a favorite target for suicide bombers, and the less time you spent skulking around them the better. Getting killed walking to school or work, that could be seen as bad luck, but walking into government buildings, that was just asking for trouble.

The Islamic State now joined the party, and between them and the Taliban, it vastly expanded the list of places to avoid. Not that we talked about the Islamic State much. IS was the new kid on the block, but we still blamed the Taliban for everything. We simplified it into a side that kills and the side that gets killed. No one really felt the need to differentiate or analyze, we left that to the outsiders looking in.

When I'd finally enter whatever ministry I was going to, it became a waiting game. No one was in any hurry to see me. Ministries were full of self-important men in ill-fitting suits, and I was about as high on their priority list as I was on a patient list in a Pakistani hospital. I'd get a number and wait, and wait, and wait.

When I was finally ushered in, official after official would dismiss me as soon as they laid their eyes on me, before I even opened my mouth. They'd dismiss me for my gender, for my age, for my obvious tribal roots.

Over and over, I came to present an idea but got lectured instead. There were times when I wouldn't get past mentioning the word "tablet." There was an initiative to give out computers to all Afghan children in 2010, and, as you can imagine, that didn't quite pan out. "We tried that, and it doesn't work." Of course it didn't work. Who on earth thought it would? The fact that the only overlap with the previous inane concept was the use of technology was lost on everyone.

Many of the officials were suspicious about the proposed content to be loaded onto the tablet, and my insistence on deviating from the established curriculum. Why did it need to be different from what they're doing? And if they weren't there to control me, what if I included something they didn't like? Arguments that children from rural areas may have different needs than the prep schools they've been setting up around Kabul were met with incomprehension.

The biggest obstacle, however, was that there was never any interest on the government's part to move away from the brick-and-mortar model. It was a winning concept as far as they were concerned: as the Taliban kept blowing up the schools as quickly as the government built them, it allowed them to turn around and ask for more money to build the same school a month later. The Taliban were not the only bandits around. We remained a broken system because too many people were profiting from the way things were. From their point of view, my insistence on change was not only stupid; it was messing with their source of income. They were happy with the ghost schools.

They'd explain it to me differently, of course. The most frequent and most infuriating counterargument was that they couldn't support my tablets because they would be taking jobs away from teachers. I quickly found out that responding with "whose jobs?" or "which teachers?" wasn't going to be well-received. I was forced to sit through the lectures full of contempt about "young people who do not understand how funds work." Or, with a thinly veiled insult to my refugee background, about not understanding "how things work in *Afghanistan*."

Hard as I tried, I couldn't figure out how to navigate the system, and trial and error got old pretty quickly. I needed a crash course in development. I needed to know how other people answered these questions before me. I decided I needed to add another internship to my schedule.

I started working for an engineering professor from Kabul University who had plenty of experience in humanitarian development, having spent years building bridges around Afghanistan. The professor happily agreed to train me, despite the fact that his work and my goals didn't overlap in the slightest. He understood that the only way for me to learn was to find those few people who weren't corrupt and latch on to them. If, in the process, I needed to learn about pine nuts and bridges, it was a small price to pay. I now had two full-time internships, both intended to help me launch my own NGO. Still, I felt like I was wasting time and getting no closer to educating the girls I was trying to help.

As my frustration was about to peak, unexpected allies started gathering in my corner. Although I was now reasonably confident that I'd be able to run an NGO, and even defend its existence to the government, there was still a sea of bureaucracy that separated me from making it a reality. Mohammad Jan, an unwitting expert in navigating said bureaucracy, offered to help.

I met Mohamad Jan at the Pine Nut Union. He was a part of the welcoming committee when I started interning there, tasked with showing me the ropes. Interns were a tight-knit group at the Union, less by choice and more by circumstance. Our hours were long, and whether we wanted or not, we got to know each other well. As a result, all my colleagues were painfully aware of my ambitions to eventually start an NGO of my own. Quite a few of them cheered me on, but Mohammad Jan went well beyond that. He sat with me after work, for hours, helping me translate my ideas into practical, tangible plans. On more than one occasion, he'd take me to his family, who would feed me. To this day I can't quite decide what I'm more grateful for: his help or his family's food.

I got another lucky break around that time. Our old boss from the Pine Nut Union graduated to a government position, landing a job with the office of the president. I suddenly had a connection within the government. He introduced me to the right people and explained the inner workings of the government approval system that had eluded me for so long.

His introductions weren't wholehearted endorsements, and mostly ran along the lines of "I'm not entirely sure what she's trying to achieve, but she works hard and comes back with results. Just let her do her thing." That sufficed, though; I was in. Suddenly my applications got stamped. I tried not to think about how many projects got approved that way, with a nod of the right official regardless of merit. I snuck into a corrupt system through the back door, and I felt like I should be grateful and not question the process. If only this once.

I finally managed to collect all the required approvals to officially register my nonprofit. I decided to call it LEARN. For the first time since turning down Oxford, I asked my father for money: I needed twenty-five dollars to register it. Mohammed Jan even drove me to the ministry to collect the certificate. No more taxis taking me halfway—I was committed to doing it in style. I entered the registration office like a boss lady.

It's the little things that keep you going.

And then, because everything always happens at once, the American University called, offering not just admission, but finally, a way to pay for it. I'd been dutifully applying every semester, waiting for a scholarship to become available. Third time was the charm: I was offered a US Embassy scholarship. I was to start school in January.

Instead of worrying about how I was going to fit it all in, the prospect of going back to school comforted me, filled me with calm. Sometimes I think that's the real reason I fight so hard for girls' education. To me, school was the only peace I knew. Maybe those girls could find some comfort there as well.

9

WITH A COLLECTION OF GOVERNMENT STAMPS in hand, I now needed to secure the tribal backing for the project. Government approval merely made my NGO official, but without the tribal endorsement, my effort to educate girls would be just another import with a short shelf life.

Community involvement was the only way to ensure a lasting change. Tribal life was the only constant in our lives for centuries and, if approached the right way, it didn't have to stand in opposition to progress nor modernity. Being a closed system, it simply required a change from within, a change that was a result of reckoning, not dictated or imposed. I thought I was well-placed to start the ball rolling. I belonged to the tribal system; I wasn't an outsider trying to prove it wrong. If anything, I wanted to prove that the outside world was wrong about us and challenge the perception that rural areas are populated with people who stayed illiterate by choice. I knew firsthand that wasn't true. They wanted to learn. They didn't lack the will; they lacked the way.

Trailing my father to tribal meetings my entire childhood came in handy. I could get easily get access to the leaders. I didn't really know what to expect, but cockily, I thought I'd be ready for whatever questions come my way.

I went to see a tribal leader deep in the Kandahar Province as a litmus test. He received me at his home, and if he was uncertain about the purpose of my visit, he didn't show it. This wrinkled, bearded man sitting across from me was probably the only person within a ten-mile radius that could read or write.

I was nervous for the first time. Ministry meetings made me defiant and angry; it was easy enough to forget about being nervous. Here, however, there was none of it. No hostility, nothing to get angry about. The stakes felt higher. My palms started sweating.

Tea was served, we exchanged pleasantries. I'm always proud when I manage not to anger anyone early in a conversation, so I saw that as a positive sign. I answered all his questions about my father's well-being at length, and then I explained why I was there. "I know there is no girls school in your village and there is no way for girls to get an education." He nodded.

"I head an NGO"—saying those words out loud still felt strange—"and the idea is to make basic education available on tablets. I would like to use them here, in Kandahar Province. That way, girls could get an education even if they're not able to go to school."

I explained that none of it was imminent; I was still waiting for the tablets to be delivered. But when they were ready, I would like to distribute them in his village. From there, I launched into explaining the technical aspect of it all. "The tablets are solar-powered, and you don't need the internet. Everything girls need is on the tablet already!" Over and over, I kept highlighting the ease of use.

I smiled as I finished with my presentation, ever so pleased with myself and my little speech. I thought it went well. It was clear and simple, informative without being condescending.

After a few seconds of silence, he asked a single question: "Why would girls need to be educated at all?"

With that, my smugness was gone.

The question wasn't a loaded one. It was simple, to the point, and relevant to the conversation. I could feel my face turning red with embarrassment and felt a sudden desire to hide. The flight response was due to the horrifying realization that I didn't know how to answer his question. To me, educating girls was about empowering them, but I knew very well that was not the argument I should offer to him. In his eyes, empowering girls was only half the answer and the less important half at that. It's what Western organizations kept getting wrong about Afghanistan. We live and breathe as a community. Individuality matters less here than in the West. Advocating for special groups is often seen as somehow less holistic, as missing the point. It's only half a pitch. If you're changing the fabric of society, you need to prove that it's for the good of the entire community. Here, the communal good reigns supreme.

I understood exactly what he meant when he asked the question, but I wasn't entirely sure how to frame my arguments in response. My pitch, the one that I was so proud of until a few minutes ago, was worse than the government proposals. At least the government came armed with the tangible benefit of bribes. I had nothing. I came to the fight unable to defend the very premise. I didn't even know how to defend education itself, not for girls, not for boys. The need for it was drummed into me, first by my own family, then the school. It was not something I ever had to formulate before. I knew instinctively that education was necessary; but knowing something instinctively is a poor starting point in a debate.

The only answers I had at the ready were those offered by my Western education, peddling degrees and advocating along the lines of furthering you career choices, which, seriously, isn't going to fly in rural Kandahar. I needed to defend getting educated as a concept not as a tool, present education as a path not as a destination. Years of working toward this conversation, and I still wasn't sure what to say. I was devastated. How did I miss that?

I faced a choice. I could try to talk my way out of it. I could offer platitudes and generic answers like a kid on an exam she didn't prepare for. Or I could acknowledge that his question was too important to wing it, admit my failure, go back to the drawing board, and figure out the actual answer. I knew walking away could easily end the conversation altogether; yet insulting him with half-baked answers somehow seemed far worse. Leaving would at least show respect, something that my little speech was apparently sorrily lacking.

I mumbled that I'd get back to him.

It took me two months to prepare the answer. I searched for religious, cultural, and practical arguments. It was my mother who trained me for this moment with her skepticism, with her cross-examination of every decision I've ever made in life. Debate clubs have nothing on a Pashtun mother hurling chaplaks at you whenever you get the answer wrong. Chaplaks significantly improve your critical-thinking abilities.

When I finally went back to see him, I quickly skipped over

the pleasantries. Yes, my father was still doing well. There was no need to get into it. I was all business. I even cleared my throat before starting.

I opened with the religious reasons: "First of all, Islam teaches us that we are meant to learn all our lives. From the cradle to the grave." I was weaving in quotes from the Quran and the hadiths that I'd memorized as supporting evidence. "Both men and women have the same obligations as Muslims. Women have to pray as often as men, they fast for Ramadan, they go to Mecca on a pilgrimage, so their obligation to learn is the same as that of men. Offering education to girls would enable them to follow the path they're supposed to, fulfill their God-given duty.

"Secondly," I continued, "women are taking care of families, and the better educated they are, the better they can do that." There was a story my mother told me a long time ago, about a woman from her family who accidentally poisoned her baby boy by giving him powdered glue instead of formula. The containers looked the same and she didn't know how to read. Her boy ended up in the hospital for three days. He recovered in the end, but she never got over almost killing her son. Teaching women like her how to read, teaching them the basics of first aid, would help them to manage the household better. "It would keep the families and our community safer.

"Lastly, the more the women know, the more they can teach their children. By educating girls, you're educating boys, too. These girls will become mothers. And educated mothers can teach their children, both girls *and* boys. Women are the key to educating the entire family." I insisted on highlighting the role of a mother for a good reason. The mother is the first and the last woman an Afghan man listens to.

See? All for the benefit of the community.

Having run out of breath, I stopped as abruptly as I started. It didn't matter, though. We were talking values now. It was content over style. He had enough information to decide.

The old man was hard to read, but I knew he listened closely. He took a painfully long time to react. He offered more tea, then more snacks, while I sat there waiting for him to respond. Maybe I deserved that agony for being unprepared the first time around, but the wait, from where I sat, still seemed unnecessarily cruel.

When he finally called it a "fine idea," I thought my head would explode.

Improbably, walking away the first time around was the right call. I realized he didn't see our conversation as a dispute. He wasn't opposed to educating girls. I wasn't an enemy; I was a partner. He just needed me to do better.

I couldn't help but think about how different the conversations with the ministries had been. The government loudly professed gender equality. We had the percentage of women ministers that rivaled the Scandinavian countries. Still, they'd never fail to let you know your place.

Now, in a rural guestroom of a supposedly backward tribal leader, there was none of that contempt. He made an effort to engage, an effort to ask questions. I may not have liked his questions, but from where he stood, they were necessary. Too often we judge people for making us defend our point of view. Yet the only questions that have the power to offend us are the ones we don't have the answer to.

When we said our goodbyes, I knew I had his full backing.

I also knew I'd earned it.

FINALLY, THE TABLETS ARRIVED. FIVE GLORIOUS, INSTALLED, CONFIG-ured, and preloaded tablets, ready to go. The first thing I did was

2002, My father, Zalmai Khan Barakzai, returning after eight months post-US invasion, to see us. I am standing on the left, my sister Sangeena is on the right, and my baby brother, Pashtoon Zalmai, sits on my father's lap.

My parents, Zalmai Khan Barakzai and Robina Zalmai.

October 2007, after my dad had resigned from his government post and returned to tribal life.

The Tomb of Ahmad Shah Durrani located in Kandahar, Afghanistan. It is the most important historical monument in Kandahar.

Sitting with my father before leaving for American University in Afghanistan.

Meeting with a tribal elder in Daman, Afghanistan to campaign for girls' education.

Training teachers in digital literacy.

My last photo with my father.

Alphabet recognition session with some young girls.

Teaching students about personal hygiene.

Presented with a peace educator mural by a partner school.

October 1, 2021, Launching our first secret school in Kandahar.

Launching my own NGO—LEARN—was a dream come true. Here I am with Giada Bleeker, a LEARN board member at an Afghans Empowered fundraiser for LEARN and other networks in Afghanistan.

take them home to show them to my original investors—my parents. Five little tablets, a payback for all those years of financing my education and tolerating my subsequent choices.

Both of my parents looked delighted, initially reluctant to even touch those cheap pieces of plastic that I put in front of them. "No, it's okay," I insisted. "They're sturdy. They're meant to be difficult to break." My mother, ever the diplomat, ran her finger around the edge of the tablet and said, "I was convinced you'd fail. I couldn't see it until now. I couldn't see it work. But I get it. I understand now."

Coming from her, it was a high praise indeed. My parents knew all too well what went into this. Convincing my reluctant mother meant more than all the ministry stamps, all the meager funds I managed to secure. For the first time, she believed that these five tablets were the start of something bigger. They gave her the confidence to respond to all the criticism directed at me, all the wondering about what I was doing with my life: "You'll see. You'll see," she was able to respond cryptically but confidently.

Still unable to pay anyone, including myself, I surrounded myself with an army of volunteers. I went straight from being an intern to having interns, most of them older than me and holding higher degrees. There was a whole new group of people to introduce the tablets to: the provincial educational director, the governor. They all hunched over the tablet with me as I explained how it worked.

Although I aimed to eventually distribute tablets in rural Kandahar, I couldn't pilot the program there right away. I had full-time school to attend. I didn't have the time to perform the necessary checks. Launching the program in rural Kandahar would require too much of my time and resources. I also needed an existing school, an existing educational program, to serve as a point of comparison. I needed an environment that had at least some familiarity with the technology, a school with at least a modicum of digital savvy. I couldn't get any of that in the rural area. My cousin introduced me to a school in the suburbs that ticked all the boxes.

Suburbs didn't fare much better than the rural areas. There, too, education was an afterthought; there were always more urgent programs to be implemented—the ones dealing with lack of running water or basic amenities. Children were dying in droves from completely preventable things. While even I, as obsessed as I was about education, couldn't argue that keeping them alive was definitely a priority, improvements were presented as an either-or. Education never quite made the cut.

Just like in the rural areas, suburb projects were all about the infrastructure. Most of those projects required a longer attention span than the government had, so they were rarely finished. Sometimes they didn't even take off. They'd be announced, the money would be allocated, and then you'd never hear about it again. Still, on paper, infrastructure was where all the government's energy and money went.

We conducted surveys, identified schools with the most severe teacher shortages, thinking they would be most likely to accept whatever help they could get. We eventually settled on piloting the program in Malajat, a suburb of Kandahar. It was a midsized, poorly funded school. Because of the proximity to the slums, they were interested in a community school type of education, painfully aware of the gaps that some of their girls needed to bridge. Initially it was my staff that kept in touch with the school, to smooth any issues teachers may have had with the tablet, but some four months later, it was midterms, and a time for a formal follow-up. I emerged from behind the mountain of paperwork for the first time since founding LEARN, to go and meet the girls. To hear what difference—if any—the tablets made. I was so eager, I got there early and had to wait for the kids to get in first. Once they were in, I somehow missed the gate closing and stayed on the outside.

It was one of those mornings.

I had just sent a text to the school administrator asking to be let in when one of the mothers ran up, dropping off a child, flustered about being late. It's a scene you can find outside any school, anywhere in the world, except for the fact that we were in the suburbs of Afghanistan.

This woman was out of breath, obviously having rushed to get here. Studying her, I suspected that she must have spent the morning making bread before sending her kids to school, for there was still some flour stuck to her garments. That's probably why she was late, I thought to myself. (I always had a strong propensity for lively conversations in my head.)

We kept silently eyeing each other while we waited for the gate to open.

As the gate keeper came out, I spoke first, saying I was there for a meeting with the principal. The mother taken aback by my appearance as much balked at hearing it. I suppose she thought I looked too young, like someone more likely to be sent to the principal than attend a meeting with him. She began talking to the gate keeper, explaining that the girl was late because of traffic. As she spoke, I could tell how proud she was to see her daughter go to school. And there was a part of me that was proud to see how much we Afghan women appreciated education and wouldn't let something as bothersome as traffic get in the way of it.

Still, this waiting annoyed me. I was already in a bad mood. The school required walking uphill, which didn't help my back pain, I didn't sleep well the night before, and I was too tired not to take it personally. When I finally walked in, I was cranky rather than nervous about the meeting.

Always a winning attitude.

The principal appeared glad to see me, but I dismissed it as him just trying to be pleasant. He appeared to be smart, and he clearly cared about his students, but I wasn't going to snap out of my bad mood that quickly: I was committed. I'm persistent that way.

He talked about how much he'd been struggling with developing the girls' imagination. "It is possibly the biggest issue we face as educators here." I nodded; I knew how hard it must be to shape minds already defeated by life. The girls were taught to look down at their shuffling feet from the moment they're born. Developing imagination requires looking up. Encouraging it requires a concrete, detailed map, not platitudes and slogans about what's achievable.

The principal walked me through the government curriculum they'd been following, written in English. He complained about the quality of teachers, an ongoing struggle in Afghanistan. Government schools only required qualified teachers beginning with the sixth grade. Before that, at the most crucial time in kids' lives, they're mostly taught by education students who have yet to graduate.

With the generic conversation now out of the way, he suddenly said that he had never seen such rapid progress as he did with my tablets. "They evened the playing field, you know? They encouraged creativity in a way I haven't seen before." As I still failed to sufficiently perk up, he suggested I should meet one of the girls and have her talk about it instead of him.

Fine.

As we walked to a classroom, it was clear that the school wasn't swimming in funds: the paint was peeling off the stained walls and the halls were full of slipshod repairs that had seen better days. Even years ago, when the improvements were undertaken, they were clearly only meant to be temporary.

When we walked in the room, the principal pointed to a girl sitting in the front row. She had beautiful hazel eyes and smiled shyly when the principal addressed her. Her eyes were bright and shining, and it was clear that she was happy. Seeing her, my mood began to shift. The principal and I sat down and the teacher showed us some of the girl's writing and pictures that she had drawn. The girl sat up straighter and beamed. She was obviously proud of her work, and I was too.

I invited the girl to sit next to me and tell me about herself. She told me that she wanted to become a painter. She said that she would draw some pictures to give me the next time I visited. I smiled and sat there imagining how great it would be in twenty years when this little girl would be an illustrator, a graphic designer, or an educator. That day ignited a hope in the future of Afghanistan that I protect to this day.

I really started paying attention in earnest once she started talking about school. She lit up. She spoke with a confidence I had never felt, not at that age, not even now. She answered my every question, perfectly self-possessed. My back pain was forgotten; the bad mood that came with it, her stains, somehow faded.

She told me where she lived, mentioning one of the poorest parts of Kandahar, without electricity or sewage; and talked about how much she liked going to school.

"I love school. You get smarter here."

It was a conversation of equals, despite her age, despite her background.

I didn't want to ask her directly about what she thought of the program. I was never scared of feedback before, but with her it was different. I couldn't bear hearing anything even remotely critical, not from her. Instead, I asked what her favorite part of the program was. It felt safer to imply that there was something about it to like.

"*The Lion King,*" she said without missing a beat, without any hesitation.

"I learned the entire *Lion King* by heart."

The principal and the teacher nodded in agreement as she said it.

"I really like how he's scared before being brave. I like how he gives up but then he fights again. But I mostly liked the pictures. Pictures are the best part."

Of course. I had included *The Lion King* in the program. He was the only Disney character I truly loved. Stories involving princesses ending up in a marriage were harder to identify with: for Afghan women, a wedding was hardly a guarantee of a happy ending; it was more of a cliffhanger—you never knew what would come next.

The Lion King was a nod to our reality: girls live in a world full of uncles trying to take what's ours. But to hear her single it out was an unexpected recognition of more than a tablet, it was a recognition of me, my efforts, my path. It brought back all those mornings I spent forcing everybody to watch *The Lion King.* I felt validated by a seven-year-old whose name I never learned.

She wasn't done talking though. "I love drawing and I'm going to be an artist one day." I wondered how a child of Afghans who always force their kids to become doctors came up with the idea to be an artist, until it finally hit me. That's what the principal was saying. It was the tablet, *The Lion King* illustrations, "the best part" of *The Lion King* that made her want to draw. That's why he introduced me to her. That's what that imagination speech was all about. I struggled to take a breath in. I've made an impact, a real, true impact on someone's life, through the program, through that tablet. I was an actual teacher now, and she was my very first student.

I was completely overwhelmed. I did the only thing I could:

I burst into tears, scaring everybody, children and teachers. Crying doesn't require an explanation in Afghanistan, no matter how sudden. There's no shortage of things to cry about. But I couldn't have explained my tears even if I tried. Her words released some invisible pressure valve. The crying incident abruptly ended the visit, but it didn't matter. We all said what needed to be said.

Elated, I didn't care that, yet again, I had no money for a cab, that it would take me hours to get home. Who needs a taxi anyway? All those times when I had to choose between developing content and getting to eat now seemed worth it. *The Lion King* girl, whose imagination I personally helped develop, was going to be an artist.

That two-hour walk home from school down the unpaved Kandahar paths seemed like a poorly attended victory parade, but it was a victory parade, nevertheless.

10

So far, running an NGO consisted of begging for approvals, followed by begging for money. Neither came naturally to me, but it was a breeze in comparison to what came next: promoting the tablet.

No one told me when I decided to start LEARN that I'd spend half of my time doing what I hated the most: speaking in public. I might be loud, and I might be opiniated, but I'm an introvert. I prefer arguing in intimate settings, and lecturing my family perched on a soapbox in my own kitchen. I've since learned to deal with public speaking, embraced it even, but back then I still had a sinking feeling in my stomach every time I had to open my mouth in front of people.

When I landed my first radio interview, I was hyperventilating for days. Getting an opportunity to talk publicly about my work was a big deal in a country oversaturated with NGOs. There were hundreds of nonprofits in Afghanistan competing for money and attention, and I was up against organizations receiving millions with nothing but five cheap tablets to show for myself. The interview was my one chance to put LEARN on the map, to convince the larger public of the worthiness of my program; I knew it was not a given that I'd get another. I talked about the need to rethink how we educate in areas outside the government reach, about my *Lion King* girl, about the needs of girls in rural areas that no one even tried to meet.

It must have gone well because a few days after that interview a message popped up in my Facebook inbox. It started with, "My father heard your interview on the radio." Someone named Hamza was saying that it took him a while to track me down, which he eventually did through a mutual friend. Although he didn't hear the interview, his father gave him a detailed account of LEARN. Hamza wrote that it seemed like a great idea and he would like to talk to me to learn more about it.

Very few people had referred to my idea as "great," so I liked Hamza already. It wasn't a fan letter though. There was potential for collaboration, he said. He added that he was the Afghanistan country director for Malala Fund. Way to bury that piece of information at the bottom of the message, Hamza.

I don't remember what I wrote to him in response. My usual eloquence failed me tragically, but given the outcome, whatever I said must have been interpreted as agreement.

When we finally met, he listened intently, which still didn't happen all that often.

What did I need?

What did I want to achieve?

Chastened by the experience of my pitch to the tribal leader, I overprepared for the meeting with Hamza. I had so many notes that it became impossible to organize them, rendering them useless. Yet again, I just talked and talked. After practicing my speech for months on so many uninterested officials, I was painfully aware that I had yet to deliver it from beginning to end, uninterrupted. Would I manage to finish this time? Did I even know how the speech ended?

Hamza wasn't my usual crowd, though. He was aware of the struggle to educate girls in rural areas; he knew they were out of reach of the uninterested government. Unlike the government officials, he didn't need to waste time being defensive about all the ways in which the education system has failed them. With varied success, it was only the NGOs that ever tried to reach them. Hamza didn't need my facts and figures; he knew them already, even those usually relegated to the fine print. He wanted to hear a bigger plan. My plan. My vision. How did I intend to use those tablets?

I explained that the tablet offered three types of content and three ways to use them.

"You could use the tablet to supplement the teaching in areas that don't have enough teachers, where the classrooms are overcrowded. The tablet offers a full curriculum so it could help not only with personnel shortages but also the occasional gaps in a teacher's knowledge." I explained that I'd been working on setting up community schools, with teachers who lack formal education and who needed all the help they could get. I wanted to plug all those holes.

"You could also use it as a resource. It could serve as a digital library in public schools where students can't afford books, and the schools don't offer any." We had a few books already on it, but I wanted to expand further. Eventually, the tablet would offer over 250 books in Pashtu, and even some in English.

"And finally," I explained, "the tablets could be used for individual and community learning. If a girl is prevented from going to school for any reason, she could just download the app once and get full access to video lectures and books."

The curriculum was skimpy at the time, but it would grow to more than three hundred lessons over time, the entire pre-K-to-12 curriculum.

I went on and on about the fact that the content needed to be downloaded only once, not because Hamza needed it explained, but as a nod to the years that I spent coming up with the solution.

What I needed, I said, was funding for more tablets and for the general costs that come with distributing them and running an NGO. During this time, a U.S. Marine named Giada Bleeker contacted me and offered to help set up a GoFundMe.

My first pitch tanked.

Despite Hamza's enthusiasm, Malala Fund was less than excited with the plan, and the pitch went the way of the hundreds of other proposals I had submitted before. It could be that my proposal writing skills were still in their infancy. I knew how to talk about it, but the finer points of grant writing were still escaping me. Most likely, however, the issue was my stubborn effort to include community schools with informally trained teachers in it. They weren't having any of it.

Luckily, Hamza was as stubborn as I was. More meetings were scheduled, and my second attempt to secure a grant from them was successful.

I now had actual funding.

Real-life money.

Used for transactions and buying things and paying people.

The kind used for getting cabs all the way to whatever school or ministry you needed to go to. Enough for a ride back, too.

As if that wasn't exciting enough, they made me Malala Fund's youngest-ever education champion just before I turned twenty-one. I thought I should mention it, as my mother's been casually dropping that fact into every conversation she's been having ever since.

Suddenly, after months of waiting for the program to take off, everything started moving at the speed of a Taliban spring offensive: stealthily, without a warning, unstoppable. More grants followed, and with them more projects.

I decided to name all the programs after Afghan heroines. That way, they came with little history lessons, with a little bit of built-in hope, a reminder that we were able to make a difference once.

It was part of a bigger plan: yes, we Afghan women had a rough few decades, but if you get to define yourself, why base self-definition on your worst days? Why not go back to when we mattered?

I remember when I was young, I would see my father's great aunt sitting in the garden with her friends: a gang of old women, impeccably dressed. These old women carried themselves differently, refusing to adjust to miserable surroundings, refusing to blend in. They stood out in every way possible. Not just with their beautiful clothes, but by the very fact that they were sitting outside, lacking servility and fear. Just imagine, in the middle of all that squalor, a gang of beautifully dressed old women smoking a hookah, discussing life. Not war, not politics, just life: land, farming, children.

They would laugh out loud, a shocking sound to hear outside a home, as it's considered inappropriate for a woman to laugh in public. Their age protected them from judgment, though; they seemed finally free. It seemed to me as if they were saying, "You see? If only you manage to live long enough, you can age out of the humiliations imposed on you for being a woman." They remembered a different existence, a life before fleeing, and they weren't going to let anyone box them in. They were irrefutable proof that you could make your own rules. Even if you are a woman.

That was what I wanted to teach the girls, too. I wanted them to know that there's more to us than—well, whatever this was. It's a lot to communicate with just a few tablets, I know, but you have to start somewhere.

I named the digital literacy program The Soraya Project, after Queen Soraya, who championed women's right to vote. With more tablets on the way, it became the driving force behind LEARN, the backbone of my NGO.

From the very beginning, though, I wanted to expand beyond just literacy. Ignoring all the other ways to learn seemed like a luxury we couldn't afford. Most people view literacy as a prerequisite for education, but that's not really the case. Nothing can be further from the truth. I have seen it: most Afghan households have radios, and you could have a decently informed conversation about foreign policy with completely illiterate people, because all they do all day is listen to BBC Pashtu. It doesn't matter if you learn Hindi from soap operas in your kitchen, in the end, it's still a skill; you still learned to speak a language. All of that can be used. There was a wealth of ways we never tapped into that could be used to educate people; why ignore them? God knows we needed all the help we could get. We needed skills far more than we needed degrees. So much knowledge can be accessed in unconventional ways, and I wanted to make use of it. Tablets ticked that box: they forced you to start thinking differently about education. Community projects were next on that list.

The government largely ignored anything unconventional,

setting up a system that never stood a chance. Their schools followed Western curriculums and, even worse, Western hours. It may seem trivial, but as the vast majority of children needed to work during the day, the hours automatically excluded millions of Afghan children too poor to choose education over income. You can rage, and you should, over child labor, but if you condition education on attendance on your terms, you're simply excluding children that need it the most. Legally banning child labor doesn't get the five-year-old off the streets and into schools. Ability to feed yourself does that. It was a vicious circle that we kept trying to break off at the wrong point: you needed to be well-off enough to go to school, and without school, you could never rise from abject poverty. Generation after generation, entire segments of society were left behind.

To be fair, this lack of creativity was partially a reflection of the system dictated by the West. The West, footing the bill, were the parents wagging their finger at the government, saying: "As long as I feed you, you need to follow my rules." The government, in response, acted like a petulant child refusing to grow up.

The last couple of decades were hardly the first time we found ourselves being dictated to. We started importing politics, educational or otherwise, swinging from one extreme to another well before that. By the time the Americans got here, we were already master importers. We've dabbled in Soviet communism and Saudi Wahabism and were by now fully trained to disregard how suitable someone else's principles might be to our way of living. Even when you repot a plant, you need to ensure that the conditions and the soil are similar. How did we get to the point where we didn't think that the same might apply to ideas?

Instead of trying to find our own solutions, we waited for the outside world to fix our broken system. We took other people's politics and then fought over them, long after the armies that brought them were gone. Afghanistan was a child of a bitter divorce of cultures, a battlefield where someone else's principles were printed on the banners of the fighting armies. We lost ourselves. In the process, we became a cannon fodder, a footnote in someone else's history. We took pride in being the "graveyard of empires," not realizing we've written ourselves out of our own obituary. We stopped thinking for ourselves.

I wanted my community projects to be a contribution to a different narrative, no matter how small. Starting community projects wasn't all strategy and altruism, mind you: talking to girls was the best part of my job, the one thing that made all that chart-making and meeting-taking worth it.

The very first project I did was on menstrual hygiene. With generations of girls married off before they even reach puberty, they knew nothing about their own bodies. They were left to figure everything out on their own.

I named the project Malalai, after a nineteenth-century Afghan heroine who, the legend has it, secured victory against the English by encouraging the tribesmen to keep fighting.

I didn't quite know what kind of reaction to expect from girls attending the menstrual hygiene course: for people who cover their women into oblivion, we Afghans are actually far less ashamed of our bodies than people in the West. We don't feel saddled by it or humiliated by its needs: people often squat outdoors when nature calls. Still, I went into the seminar expecting what I've seen in Hollywood movies, in which any attempt to discuss one's body produces giggles and discomfort.

There was none of that. The general eagerness in the class was shocking: all those twelve- and thirteen-year-olds asking endless questions, thrilled to take pictures with me for LEARN's website. They all wanted to be a part of it.

I insisted on getting them goodie bags, the kind you get when you attend the real, grown-up seminars, but I only had money for the bags themselves. The girls didn't care that the bags were empty, though. They happily pranced around with their seminar totes, delighted that there was a gift for them at all. I didn't quite know if I should be excited or devastated by how grateful they were for my attention.

With the piloting done, it was time to sink or swim. I decided to take the tablets to my district. The first lot went to Zarghona and Nazo, whom I now folded into LEARN.

Well, sort of.

The two still couldn't receive their salaries from LEARN because I never got the funding for them. Like my father some thirty years ago, I just couldn't explain the idea of leaving education in the hands of women who weren't formally educated. On paper, .qualified teachers existed in rural areas, drawing government salaries. It didn't matter that they were sitting at home because the schools where they were supposed to teach didn't exist. My program nominally downgraded the requirements for teaching for no reason at all. It didn't matter that government schools were an educational equivalent of Narnia. On paper, I just couldn't compete.

Having failed repeatedly to secure salaries for Zarghona and Nazo, it seemed prudent to limit my funding requests to one crazy idea at the time, so I stuck with requesting funding for the tablets only. I wanted everything to be aboveboard. Since I had a salary now, I was able to pay them myself.

My failure to convince anyone that these women were worth funding turned Zarghona and Nazo into a project. Out of sheer desperation, I started a teacher program for them, training women to be digital educators, hedging an approved digital curriculum to compensate for the lack of formal credentials. I couldn't give them degrees, but I could offer certificates.

Ayesha Durrani, who was an eighteenth-century poetess,

seemed like a perfect anchor for the teacher training program. Her poems were compiled into one of the first books ever printed in Afghanistan, and she was credited by some with opening the first school for girls. The blend of schooling and poetry circles that she invoked was irresistible.

For now, the only community aspect of the digital learning program was a little projector distributed with each tablet. That way, girls would at least be able to learn in groups. Tablet content was, to say the least, eclectic: I tried to cover as much ground as possible, for as diverse an audience as possible. There were lessons on everything, from the basics of writing to instructions on how to sell your embroidery on Facebook. And *The Lion King*, obviously. *The Lion King* was nonnegotiable; they were going to get rid of it over my dead body. It was included in everything. I was happy to explain and defend the purpose of every video, every lesson we offered. Not *The Lion King*, though. It stayed because I said so.

The plan, tweaked and adjusted daily, was starting to look almost coherent. I, too, was getting more attention, although I still wasn't entirely sure how to capitalize on it.

Kabul had a lively nonprofit social scene. There were dinners to attend every other night, but I was too busy with work and studies and further hampered by the general lack of interest in socializing. I ignored mass invitations, but I'd respond to those who reached out to me personally.

Sarah was one of those people. She sent me a private message on Instagram. "It would be lovely if we could get together to discuss your efforts." Seeing the message gave me a pause. Sarah was a NATO coordinator for engagement with civil society, the umbrella under which all the NGOs fell.

Kabul developed tolerance for interactions with NATO; it was commonplace for the military and the NGOs to mingle. In rural areas, however, there was still apprehension; there were a lot of civilian drone deaths to get over. But Sarah wouldn't let up: "I find it fascinating, what you're trying to do with LEARN. I really want to know more about the program." Flattery about LEARN, always the best approach, finally made me grudgingly agree to meet her.

Sarah invited me to a function at the NATO base, and although nothing kills your street cred more quickly than galivanting around a NATO base, for some reason I went. I was promptly punished for my initial lack of enthusiasm about meeting Sarah: she became an instant friend. Meeting her felt more like a reunion than an introduction.

Soon we had standing coffee appointments. One day, I arrived utterly frustrated with my community school efforts, worn down by yet another failed attempt to secure funding for the teachers. It was one of those epic rants: "There are two hundred and seventy thousand employees on the Ministry of Education's payroll, and they're happy to fund schools that don't exist and teachers that don't teach, but God forbid they get behind a concept that is clearly working." I reward all my friends with random rants.

Sarah patiently listened, unable to get a word in. "I have no advice for you," she said eventually, "but . . ." It was one of those "buts" where the pause is so long you keep wondering if the sentence will ever end. "But," she said again, just in case I missed it the first time, "maybe I could contribute to the teacher salaries? Me, personally? As a private citizen?"

I don't know whether she did it out of shared frustration or in an effort to simply shut me up; both reasons would have been equally valid. But. But. The amount she mentioned was enough to open one more school.

By our next outing Sarah talked her own mother into funding another school.

Now there were three of us paying teachers out of our own pockets. This was practically a control group! I was hoping it would help with the credibility of the program, that people would finally be able to judge it based on results.

I was immensely proud of the fact that I was creating jobs for women, even if I was the one paying them, even if I couldn't convince a single organization that it was a good idea. Seeing Zarghona and Nazo blossoming, seeing their pride at being employed—we finally moved on from headscarves—I knew that work for women was about far more than establishing earning ability. Career may be too strong a word—yet—but employment presented women in a different light: as experts at certain things within their own community.

It felt like I was working off a list that I started compiling when I was a child. One by one I was addressing the needs of every girl I crossed paths with in my childhood: those married off at nine because of the crippling poverty, those in villages that had no schools, or those who couldn't walk to school because of polio even when there was one. I knew I was too late to help my friends, but what I was trying to do was done in their name. They were the heroines from my personal history, to me, no less important than the heroines from our collective past.

For the longest time, it seemed I was nothing but a bad example, an investment without return, bringing shame to my family. Now I was a proof that an investment in a girl's education can pay off. My father could be proud of me. I was not a cautionary tale anymore.

11

F EW AFGHANS PAID ATTENTION TO THE REPORTS
of the unknown virus in China. The general
consensus was that, surely, there was nothing
for us to worry about; not even a virus could
thrive in Afghanistan. Instead, we just watched
in wonder as the world shut down, city by city;
we watched as everybody's roaming space got reduced to that of an Afghan woman: a kitchen,
bedroom, maybe a backyard if you're lucky. All
these decades of trying to catch up to the world,
and now improbably, the world started resem-
bling us.

Initially the government, somewhat half-heart-
edly, tried to warn people about the dangers of
congregating. They knew the chances of anyone

heeding their warnings were pretty slim, whatever the message. There was no lockdown, but the government figured that the next best thing would be a curfew, so they instituted one from 8:00 a.m. to 4:00 p.m. It practically ensured that everybody went out at the same time, increasing rather than decreasing the chances of COVID spreading. As dumb as that was, the curfew doesn't even make the top ten of the deadliest government decisions. Even the Taliban tried to be socially responsible and suddenly stately, allowing the health workers to access areas under their control—an unexpected first. It didn't take long for all to go back to their old habits, however: the government returned to embezzling aid—COVID aid offered new funds to pillage, and the Taliban went back to securing more territory. For the rest of us, worrying about dying of COVID didn't even make it to the qualifying round anyway.

By the end of March of 2020, schools and universities shut down and my projects came to an abrupt halt. No one thought it would last, so it felt like a gift, an opportunity to come up for air, a chance to finally spend more time with family. For me, the added bonus was that my family was staying in Kandahar, where my brother was undergoing a crash course in managing our land and our vineyards.

But then, it all blew up in earnest.

Tribal areas were hit hard, although the figures don't show it. They stopped testing fairly quickly: tests had to be sent to Kabul, and by the time they returned, most of the patients would be dead. The entire exercise of testing was helpful only as a statistic—and a misleading one at that, as there were not nearly enough tests to get an accurate picture.

The entire population fell into the high-risk category: most Afghans have lingering health issues or pre-existing conditions, crushed under the weight of stress and plagued by malnutrition. It doesn't take much to knock us down.

When my father, my indominable, fate-defying father got sick, we all thought it was just one of the many health issues he kept struggling with. We have a family history of kidney disease and so we all promptly blamed it on his kidneys. He had grown pale, he couldn't eat. The Kandahar doctor checked him out and declared it a digestion issue. We weren't so sure. Even my mother, with her lifelong belief that any issue short of a severed limb is, indeed, just your stomach demanding fiber, wasn't convinced his issues had anything to do with the digestion. His loss of appetite was severe, his energy plummeted. Each family member now had his or her own version of what was wrong with him, and despite the pandemic raging all around us, not one of us thought of COVID. We tiptoed around the house, and my mother would sit on the bed next to him, covering him in cold towels to bring his fever down.

It was the month of Ramadan, when we fast from sunset to sundown. Iftar, the meal that breaks the fast in the evening, is always a family affair. There was no ignoring how weak my father grew once he stopped joining us for iftar. He couldn't stand or sit or eat anymore. He wasn't even able to stomach the bread with yogurt that my mother prepared for him, an Afghan dish that you feed to babies and the sick. No matter how hard we all tried to ignore the gravity of the situation, sitting to eat without him finally made us realize it was time to get him to the hospital, a bigger one, with better diagnostics than the one in Kandahar. He needed to go to Pakistan.

I had an exam coming, with my least favorite professor, so it was decided that I would stay behind in Kandahar to study. It was pointless to argue otherwise: neither my illnesses nor anyone else's would ever be reason enough to interrupt education. "Death may qualify as a justifiable reason, but only your own." I've heard it often enough; I knew better than to try to even broach the subject of going with them.

It was my mother and brother who took my father to Quetta, which turned out to be only the first stop. His kidneys were starting to fail, and as they had no machines for dialysis there, they transferred him to Karachi.

The hospital there, however, refused to admit him. The doctor took one look at my father and said it was COVID. Then he took another look at my family's tribal attire and refused to allow him into the hospital.

This wasn't unusual, not in Afghanistan, and definitely not in Pakistan; hospitals would often refuse to admit people with COVID, so they wouldn't infect the others. They claimed there was not enough equipment, so there was no point; why allow the sick in at all? But they weren't running out of beds; they were just even more selective than usual about who they would give them to. My father apparently didn't merit one.

My mother—wisely—decided not to share with me the news about them refusing to admit my father, knowing I'd probably try to start a war with Pakistan over it. They didn't need my help, though. Karachi is full of Pashtuns with connections to our tribe, and my father was their champion. There were plenty of people who had a family member that was at one point or another helped by my father.

The word spread fast, and Karachi Pashtuns descended on the hospital. Nominally a vigil, their presence in large numbers also made a none-too-subtle point about admission. As even COVID is preferable to a possible Tarozai-Kandahari riot, the hospital finally relented and admitted my father.

There is avoidance in our culture to deliver bad news. Obviously, we're not shy about confrontations and escalate them to shootings more often than not; but delivering bad news is considered impolite, as if discussing them openly somehow imparted a lack of kindness. We say everything is going to be okay, even when all the evidence points to the contrary. In fact, especially if all the evidence points to the contrary.

Therefore, in line with that time-honored tradition, it was a family decision not to tell my father that he had COVID.

It led to some awkward moments.

Once admitted, my father wanted to show his appreciation for the support he received, insisting on a procession of tribesmen so he could personally thank them for helping him get admitted. An immaculate host that he always was, my father kept encouraging everybody to come closer, as a way of bestowing honor, utterly annoyed with my mother's apparent and inexplicable lack of social graces. She kept visitors at the door and, what's worse, refused to offer them juice as is customary, saying that she served all of them juice in the hallway already and that they didn't need any more juice.

She believed, and rightfully so, that the best way of thanking the people was not to get them infected.

My family, however, still sat with him. Contagious or not, my mother refused to leave his side, listening to him talking about the lack of family unity, promising to reunite the family once and for all because the discord and the feud were hurting our name. My father's hospital hours were filled with talk about healing the rift: he was going to talk to them, explain it better.

My father was about to be transferred to intensive care, and they all wanted to make sure he ate something first. My brother went to get him a pudding. My father insisted he couldn't eat anything, but my brother teased him, calling him a coward, saying that eating a hospital pudding is the ultimate test of any man's courage. My father laughed and conceded, and ate some of that tasteless, neon-colored blob of sugar.

That was to be his last meal. Then, he asked my brother if he could bring him his shaving kit. "I want to be clean before they take me to the ICU."

With my brother's help, he cleaned up, took a shower, and put on a clean, starched white tribal dress. Washed and clothed, he sat on the bed.

That's when he collapsed.

They immediately rushed him to the ICU. He wasn't able to breathe on his own anymore. My mother and brother sat outside the ICU, ambushing medical staff on their way out, begging for updates.

My brother was now in charge of signing forms, making decisions about whether my father should live or die. He wasn't even eighteen yet, but he was my father's male heir and that trumped anything my mother had to say. As soon as he was presented with the first form, a gigantic bill to keep my father alive, he called me.

I didn't hesitate: "Sign it. Just sign for everything, and if there's an experimental treatment, sign him up for that too." Money didn't matter; we would think about that later. I knew my father was planning on getting a new car, and he was going to buy a new computer for me, so there was money at home. The pandemic slowed everything down, including my finances, and I was happily accepting gifts and donations from the family for the first time in years. I was certain that we had access to enough money to pay his hospital bills—for now, anyway.

Through all this, I was more concerned about my brother having to deal with this at so young an age than for my father's health. My brother would call me, saying how his hands kept shaking signing those forms, and all I could think of was how terrible it must be for him; he was still a child. It seems incredible looking back, that not one of us even contemplated my father dying at the time. Why should we? My father always came back.

The doctors seemed to suggest the same. Yes, they conceded that he was in a coma, but they portrayed it as a temporary state, reversible, as if all we needed to do was wait it out.

So we waited. For thirty-six days my mother just sat in the green painted corridors of the hospital, waiting for the miraculous recovery she'd been promised.

The first couple of weeks, I was blissfully unaware of what was going on. We spoke several times a day, but my mother parroted the doctors' words: he's in a coma and he's doing fine. It went on until I got angry and pointed out that the two were mutually exclusive; he could either be in a coma or he could be fine. Fed up, I finally headed to Pakistan. Borders were closed because of COVID, but that's fixable with a little determination and a whole lot of bribes.

When I reached the hospital, I busted the doors open like a cowboy in an old Western and headed straight for the ICU. I needed to get an update from the doctors, the same lot that wouldn't admit my father, and I was determined not to allow them to dismiss me the way they dismissed my mother or my underage brother. I started yelling. I yelled a lot. It always seemed like I had to make my voice louder than the rest, to make up for being a woman, for being an Afghan, for being tribal.

I demanded to see the doctor, and after some initial resistance, the hospital staff must have realized that it would be easier to just give in than to deal with me, so they called one. The doctor tried to sound reassuring, but I was having none of it. I insisted on seeing my father's tests.

At some point, I should probably stop modeling my behavior after American movies, but that day I channeled every legal drama I ever watched. Reserve your judgment: movies are the only place I've seen people stand up for themselves. "I'm going to file a case against you and the entire hospital if anything happens to him, unless you tell me what's going on." I wasn't even sure if one could sue a hospital in Pakistan, but that was irrelevant.

The doctor's response, patronizingly, started with "Listen, sister," prompting me to point out our lack of relation, as well as my general lack of desire for one. I wasn't there to bond with him, I just wanted to know what was happening to my dad.

And so he told me.

"Your father is not likely to wake up. We expect him to stay in a coma for the rest of his life." And they didn't expect it to be a long life, either. His coma wasn't a temporary state from which he would miraculously wake up one day, the way they explained it to my mother. They were waiting for him to die. "Just leave him here at the hospital; he's cared for here."

That couldn't be right, I thought. He clearly doesn't know my father. I started calling family, trying to find a way to get a second opinion, preferably a non-Pakistani one. My own experience with Pakistani doctors was hardly pleasant, and I refused to trust them to judge my father's condition. Especially since they were so obviously wrong. What do you mean "He isn't going to wake up?"

We found a doctor in India, and I submitted all of my father's tests and charts to him. His advice was to take my father out of the hospital. "He isn't being treated at all. Ask for an EEG, and if there's no activity, just take him home. They're just taking your money. What you need is a ventilator, they should hook him up to it there and then just take him home. At least he'll be with you." As I listened to him, I ignored the confirmation that my father's state could not be reversed and concentrated instead on the plan of action he proposed. I hated feeling helpless, and this gave me something to do: find a ventilator

When I hung up, it suddenly dawned on me just how serious all of this was. We were losing him. *I* was losing him. I don't know how we managed to delude ourselves for so long. How does thirtysomething days of someone being in a coma in the ICU, hooked up to machines, not prepare you for the idea of their death? But I just didn't see it as a possibility.

I kept my composure long enough to request an EEG, as the Indian doctor advised, and then I went back to my sister to tell her about this latest conversation. Walking down those corridors, something broke in me, and by the time I reached her, I couldn't speak. The right side of my mouth was paralyzed; I looked like I was having a stroke. It was as if I physically refused to utter the possibility of my father dying.

The paralysis just kept getting worse until the rest of my body caught up and I couldn't move at all. In the end, they admitted *me* to the hospital. It took me a day to regain movement. I tried to get my father's results, but the doctor was gone for the day and the staff insisted we wait until the next morning. No amount of bullying would change their minds, so I finally conceded. I had plenty of stuff to organize; I needed an air ambulance to take my father to Kandahar. Hours on bumpy roads would do him no good; I wanted him to be as comfortable as he possibly could be.

Not even an hour after we left, we got a call from the hospital telling us to go back.

It didn't sound like a call about test results.

We rode in silence.

The doctor waited until we had gathered around him, stated my father's name, paused, and said with all the solemnity he could muster: "He is no more. He has left this world."

This time, I didn't lose my voice. I started screaming before the doctor even finished speaking, trying to drown out his voice and his words. I kept screaming until my brother's face came into focus, pleading with me, begging me to stop. I was scaring everybody. My brother kept saying that my father would have objected to this, to my desperation, to my refusal to accept. It took a while for his words to process.

In Afghanistan, losing a father makes you an orphan. Mothers don't count because of the social structures, because they have little ability to provide for the children, because they themselves have so few rights. In my case, the sense of being orphaned wasn't culturally preconditioned. My father felt like my whole world.

I only became aware of my surroundings when I saw my brother faint. I closed my mouth and finally stopped screaming, shocked into compliance by the sense of responsibility. I do responsibility well. I went to tend to my brother. When he came to, I picked him up and took him outside. We sat on the bench outside the hospital and I told him what a horrible loss it was, to lose a father, especially one like ours, one who's kind, one who always fought for us. I comforted him, the best I knew how. Unlike me, he was still a child. Like a proper Pashtun, I kept saying we were going to be okay, never believing a word of what I was saying myself.

The hospital initially refused to release my father's body. It was an almost welcome distraction: I jumped at an opportunity to fight. The idea of my father's body in an unmarked mass grave trumped even my despair over his death.

With his body finally in an ambulance, we headed to Kandahar.

There were no more tears. My father always objected to mourning in public. I don't know if it's because the tribal norms dictate dignity, or because Islam advocates surrender to God's will, or just all those years spent fighting. To my father, accepting death without a complaint was a matter of honor. I held my tears back and insisted that the rest of the family should do the same. There will be no crying at his feet.

An Islamic funeral consists of the washing of the body, wrapping it in a white cloth, and a communal prayer before the body is laid to rest.

I stood outside as my brother helped to wash our father's body. Just before they take a person to be buried, you get to see the body for the last time.

I refused to go into the room where my father's body was.

"You need to see him," my aunt said. I shook my head no, repeatedly, until she took me by the hand and guided me into the room. Everything in me resisted entering that room, I was resisting every step I took. If I never saw his dead body, I could still pretend he was alive.

It's a moment you're meant to let him go, say your goodbyes.

I'm not sure if anyone ever rises to the occasion, but I certainly didn't. I refused to look at his face. I didn't have the courage to see it lifeless. Instead, I put my hand on his neck. I couldn't distract myself from the coldness of his body. I noticed he had a white beard; didn't realize his hair had turned gray in ICU. I wasn't there for it. I wasn't there for him. None of us were.

I was suddenly reduced to feeling like a five-year-old, wanting to reach for my father's hand. I didn't know how to live without him. My father was my guiding light, my moral support, and my spine. He was my love.

I was the last person in, and then they came to pick him up and take him to the burial site, with my brother leading the procession. My sister, who didn't go to see him, screamed as they started carrying him out. My mother fainted. I did nothing, I said nothing. I looked out to the backyard, full of people paying respects.

My brother later told me that when they brought my father's body to the family cemetery, there were over five thousand men in attendance—and one woman. She somehow made her way there, despite the fact that women aren't allowed anywhere near the burial site. The woman was old, and sobbing inconsolably, so no one tried to stop her. The men reluctantly paused the funeral proceedings and allowed her to see my father's body wrapped in the burial cloth. She put her hand on the cloth, her eyes closed, completely still. The men, too, just stood there, waiting for her to finish whispering her prayers. Then she walked away.

Everybody assumed the old lady was a relative who just missed the wake, so one of my cousins followed her to thank her for coming and extend the invitation to see the family.

She declined, saying that she wasn't related to us and that she couldn't possibly go. "Why then," my cousin asked, "did you come?"

"It was thirty years ago that I lost my husband in the war. I ended up on the street with my children, begging. I had nowhere to go." My father, whom they had never met before, happened upon them and took her and her children in. Wiping her tears she said, "When I heard he died, I wanted to thank him one more time for his kindness. I wanted God to know how grateful I was."

Although no one there remembered her, no one doubted the story was true. Kindness was the measure of my father's life.

Even more fitting, however, was the fact that a woman crashed his funeral. I thought about how much my father would have appreciated that; I could almost hear him laugh at the idea. Never one to miss an opportunity to make a point, I imagined my father saying with a smile: "See? I told you. All it takes is one woman and you can turn things around."

12

MOURNING IN AFGHANISTAN IS RESERVED FOR the wife, and the wife alone. Like any other custom applicable to women, being in mourning is about restricting movement: the wife is confined to the house for four months and ten days after her husband's death. Choosing where my mother would mourn had long-lasting implications, although we didn't know that at the time. Given the uneasy relationship with the uncles on my father's side, having her mourn at the house in Quetta, where we'd share the house with them, didn't sound like a great idea.

Instead, we took my mother to our home in Kandahar city and settled there. It would be easy for me to go to Kabul from there once school resumed, and it was the best place for my brother to continue with his now accelerated training in tribal affairs. In Kandahar, we could all stay together.

With my brother still being underage, with my mother confined to the house, I was now in charge of family affairs: finances, the education of my sister and my brother, my mother's well-being.

It was my brother who was, both culturally and religiously, considered my father's heir. He was the one who'd carry our name forward, the one expected to continue to lead not just the household but the tribe. Customarily, being a man, he would have been the one who'd inherit most of my father's estate.

Not in our family.

I must have been fifteen when my father mentioned in passing his intention to follow the standard inheritance rules and leave the majority of the estate to my brother. It was discussed only once, but that one conversation sufficed.

True to form, the moment he mentioned the traditional division, I exploded. "You treated me like a son your entire life! But now, now I get to be a daughter?" I wasn't going to let him downgrade me now.

"Are you trying to punish us for being girls? You raised me to be an equal, you raised my sister to be an equal, you have to honor it now! If someone like you doesn't fight it, who will? How can we be anything but defeated if even *you* aren't willing to fight it! You cannot do things by half! You cannot falter now."

That was the gist of my very, very long speech, delivered at full volume.

My father was thoroughly amused by my outburst. The strangest things made him beam with pride, and my outrage about the inheritance was one of them. The rest of the family—my mother, brother, and sister—rolled their eyes, not at the content, but, as usual, at my delivery.

My brother tried to chime in, attempting to agree with me, but I quickly silenced him: "You're not allowed to speak. You're just a baby." I'd gladly lay my life down for both of my siblings, but that didn't mean that I was willing to listen to what some ten-year-old had to say on a subject. Any subject. Even if he was agreeing with me.

It was suspicious how promptly my father caved in. Too readily he agreed that everything should be divided equally, as if it wasn't that big a deal at all, as if he didn't say the exact opposite just minutes ago. I've wondered ever since whether that whole conversation was nothing but a test, a way to discuss our lives after his death without worrying us, a way to confirm everybody's rights and expectations. We all knew that winding me up was always the quickest and surest way to find out.

After that, my father would bring up the decision to split the estate equally between the three of us every chance he got. In our culture, your intentions have to be announced, and publicly naming your successors carries more weight than a written will. I realize now that he talked about it as much as he did because he suspected that the written will might be contested. By constantly talking about it, he preemptively secured dozens of witnesses to his decision within the tribal community and the extended family. When talking to his friends, he'd add, with great pleasure, that he was doing it mostly because he got yelled at by his daughter. As I keep saying, he was a strange man.

For our extended family, his will was yet another point of contention. We belong to the Tarozai-Barakzai Durrani tribe, the biggest Afghan tribe that yielded influence throughout our history. The khan's will and testament is far more than just a division of assets. It's a division of power. Whoever inherits the title of Khan could claim the part of the inheritance that comes with the position. By adding the girls to his will, my father deemed the prospect of my uncles rising to the position of khan dramatically less likely. If his estate is divided equally between the three children, the brothers would be completely sidelined, without any hope of eventually inheriting any part of my father's estate.

Most of the family feuds were prompted by adding me into the family dynamics. Although my leadership prospects were seen more as an annoyance than an actual possibility, it became a matter of principle. Why start bringing women into the picture now? It was selfish and ill-advised. The rest of them secured enough sons. As far as they were concerned, I was already involved in more things than I ever should have been. I thought too highly of myself. Not only did I have opinions, which was bad enough by anyone's standards, but I was willing to share them. Publicly. And don't even get them started about all that money spent on my education.

I picked up on my family's displeasure early. Growing up, I'd poke the bear and talk to my cousins about becoming a khan as a way to try to rattle my annoyingly unflappable brother and irritate the extended family. It was contrariness, mostly, as I had no interest in the position. I wanted the possibility of being considered for the title, rather than the title itself. I didn't want to be dismissed just because I was a woman.

My father's reluctance to admit that a woman could never be seriously considered for leadership didn't help. He insisted that Afghans had women khans before, but even I wasn't entirely convinced that was true. My father, who could usually recite dates and figures from Afghan history from memory, couldn't name a single woman khan even when pressed. Sure, we had queens before, but they were married to kings. They were half of a power couple. We even had women warlords, but that definitely didn't count. Afghans would listen to anyone who's armed. But a woman leading a tribe? Nah.

Still, there was no dissuading my father; he stubbornly persisted that there was nothing in religious or tribal rules that prevented women from leading.

His side of the family was already wary of precedents. My father became the khan despite the fact that he was only the fourth-born—already a point of resentment for his brothers. Khans may be determined by lineage, but there's a process of approval. The position isn't simply hereditary: the lineage makes you a candidate, but not necessarily an heir. My father was named as his successor by his father, but it was down to tribal leaders to decide and pledge allegiance.

During his life, my father significantly expanded the family's influence. Because of our refugee status, many at the camp were left out of their tribal structure and came to Pakistan unrepresented. Eventually, they all integrated under my father's leadership. A lot was at stake.

When my father died, it didn't even occur to me to challenge the status quo. His dying wish was that the family would get reunited, and I was determined to respect it.

Before we even buried my father, I went to my uncle, the same one who tried to yank me out of school when my father was in prison, and asked him to manage tribal affairs until my brother was old enough.

"My father loved you so much. I want to put our personal history behind. We should get past the rivalry, focus on the family and the name and the legacy." Like any clan, we already had enough enemies and tribal feuds, we didn't need internal struggles, too.

"I want to continue my work with LEARN, but I promise that I'll keep helping with my brother's training. I will get him ready to take over. You won't have to do it for long."

My uncle promptly agreed, adding I should just get married

and settle down. "If you had a husband, the people wouldn't bother you with tribal issues." As soon as he brought up marriage, I should have realized that the conversation was taking a very different turn, but I wasn't able to fully process his response. I walked away feeling strange about his words, about his phrasing, but the actual meaning still escaped me.

I should have paid more attention. Within three days of burying my father, my uncle claimed my father's turban, signifying the leadership of the tribe, the turban that was meant to go to my brother. It was a claim to khanship, not a temporary measure. He did so without consulting either us or the tribal elders. He did so without any necessary procedures, or the elaborate ceremonies required, without being accepted by anyone as a leader, without any of the tribesmen pledging allegiance to him.

He just took my father's turban and promptly left Afghanistan, leaving the tribe he was supposed to lead behind.

That was just the beginning.

A day later, he and the rest of my uncles laid claim to all of my father's land, to all of our properties, to all of my father's personal belongings. Not just the ones that come with the position of the khan, but everything we owned. Our entire inheritance. They denied us access to our own land, our own vineyards where my father taught my brother how to tend to grapes. They denied us access to the family compound in Quetta that my father built, where my father invited his brother to live after they returned from Canada and had nowhere to go. The only thing they left us with was the house in Kandahar city where my mother was in mourning. Apparently, dragging out my freshly widowed mother, kicking and screaming, was where they graciously decided to draw the line.

They contested my father's will on the basis that it is inappropriate for a woman to inherit. Adding insult to injury, most of my uncles spent their adult lives in the West, readily upholding gender equality inside their own homes. Yet they were apparently still Afghan enough to know that here they could steal from women and children with impunity.

I was in a daze. I just lost my father. I was struggling to keep my head above water, unable to think beyond where I was going to find money for my sister and my brother to continue their education, having just spent a fortune on my father's treatment. I now had a lengthy legal fight ahead of me, which in Afghanistan could take years. How would I educate them in the meantime? Never mind educating them . . . how would I feed them?

My uncles' actions felt like far more than just theft. It felt like they were intent on erasing my father's name, denying him his legacy.

An even more horrifying realization was that it was down to me to protect it. Not just my father's legacy, but my brother's future leadership. All of that was down to me now.

I tried to recruit the tribesmen for help. They started reposting pictures of me and my father on tribal pages on Facebook as soon as he passed away, and I thought I could plead my case with them. Seeing those pictures meant the world to me; reading the captions saying I was continuing my father's work was a rare source of comfort. I thought they were messages of support for what was stolen from us. I thought my continuation of his work was meant figuratively. I thought it was a nod to my work with LEARN, about all the projects that I was doing in the community.

Oh, how I misread it.

It was none of that.

It was a campaign.

The tribe, unlike my uncles, respected my father's wishes for the khanship to stay in our family, and my uncle's swift exit from

Afghanistan only reinforced their belief. Given no choice of an eligible male heir, I was apparently tapped to be the next in line. It's amazing, the things you can find out on Facebook.

I didn't take it seriously. How could anyone take any Facebook posts seriously, let alone the ones suggesting a woman should lead a Pashtun tribe? No matter what my father used to say, tribal leadership was always firmly in the hands of men. I had college exams to deal with, I had an NGO to run, I didn't have time for their elaborate jokes. I was struggling and failing everybody already. More than anything else, I was in mourning for my father, my light, the love of my life. What did they want from me? I lost my father's inheritance because my own family refused to allow a woman to inherit; it was inconceivable that the tribe would even consider me for the position of khan.

Wasn't it?

I suppose I have been by my father's side since I was a child. I suppose it was easy to remember us; my father and I were always such a ridiculous sight: he in his tribal attire, with his cape and turban; me in my jeans and ratty T-shirts, forever trailing behind him. For years he'd been asked, "Why do you always take the girl with you?" Time after time, my father would let it be known that he took offense to me being called the "girl." "She's my *child*." It wasn't the semantics. It's a distinction few outside Afghanistan could ever understand, but here, it made a world of difference. My father knew his people well. The label of "child" and not "girl" apparently made me an exception to the rule in the eyes of the tribe, and this gave me a head start. I was already in the public sphere, not a space that was easily granted to a woman. I realized, just as I did when I was starting LEARN, that I already knew everyone. For years, I sat with the tribal leaders, I ate with them, I drank tea with them. They knew I opened a community school in Spin Boldak, they knew I distributed tablets in villages. They knew all of that because I went to them for permission. They certainly knew I was willing to fight. After all, I fought with quite a few of them, too.

Maybe they weren't joking after all. The tribe needed an advocate for their community. Tribal life is brutal. We're on the outside of government interest on both sides of the border, and without the community support and leadership, people are helpless. They don't have a voice of their own. It's a khan's job to ensure they're heard; that they, too, count for something. Now, without my father, who was there to protect them? My uncle, who thought that being a khan was all about accessorizing with a turban?

Being a khan is like trying to plug leaks in a dam with nothing but a kid-size shovel at your disposal. It's a thankless job because you know from the very beginning that you won't be able to solve it all, or even most of it. You just have to keep going and do your best.

I had quizzed my father about every subject under the sun, yet it never even occurred to me to ask why he chose to stay in the refugee camp when all of his brothers went abroad. I already knew the answer. The camp was his community, those that lived there were his people. The sense of responsibility for your people grounds you in more ways than one.

I inherited my father's desire to help, his passionate love for our community. My uncles only saw the outward signs of the position: his hand being kissed; his judgment being heeded. I could even understand them not noticing my father's agony over the conditions our community lived in. But what I couldn't forgive was that they didn't seem to know just how much he'd done for that community.

I came to realize that the tribe remembered that I too did what I could for them. Granted, the projects I undertook were small: from food drives to fixing gates, they were just side issues that I've encountered working on LEARN projects. But, neglected by all, the tribe's bar for doing good wasn't that high anyway.

Too busy with my own internal battle over self-value and the general standing of women in the world, I kept missing all the subtle clues, all the tribal crumbs that were left to show me the way. Someone needed to spell it out to me. My father's dearest, oldest friend cut to the chase, "You should take on your father's role."

He insisted I should start meeting people and finally respond to the tribal demands. Although not entirely convinced, I agreed, partly out of respect for him, but mostly because I still thought that any engagement with the tribal leaders would help us recover the property that was taken.

After days of drinking green tea with various tribal representatives, I realized that not one of them was willing to get involved in what they saw as a family affair. My pleadings were dismissed with: "Eh, it's a family matter, and you don't really need anyone's help. You'll eat them alive. You're strong." Then they proceeded to talk about me taking over the leadership of the tribe.

Okay then.

I had a condition of my own. I wanted to make sure they all understood that my leadership would be temporary, and that my brother would take over as soon as he was old enough, and that at the end of the day, their allegiance would be not just to me, but to my brother, too. Once they agreed to that, bewildered, I started working on my candidacy.

Normally, accepting a new khan comes with a long list of ceremonies, ending in the turban being passed on, sealing the deal. The fact that the turban was stolen was a blessing in disguise. It didn't require figuring out how to change the tradition: as a woman, I couldn't have worn it anyway. My white headscarf would have to do. The one my father gave me before going to Afghanistan was in tatters, but I kept getting new ones. Always white, like Khan Bibi's.

I found everything that was happening around me surreal: from losing the inheritance *because* I was a woman, to being offered tribal leadership *despite* being one.

Still, nothing came as a bigger shock than young men in their twenties and thirties expressing their support for my leadership. I met a lot of tribal elders over the years through my father, but my encounters with younger men were far less frequent. The last I remembered of them was me battling it out on the dusty grounds of the refugee camp back when they were still awkward preteens with their guns and contempt for girls. When did that change? They were suddenly respectful, with old friends addressing me as Khan Pashtana, which I found funny to no end, and occasionally giggle-inducing.

Strangely, it was their respect that I found most reassuring. They were the new generation, my generation, and they didn't find the idea of a woman leading a tribe strange. It was their acceptance of me that was my father's true legacy.

I quickly found out that being a woman leader had one major issue that needed to be resolved. Despite all the respect they were showing, it seemed like every single tribesman felt entitled to offer plenty of completely unsolicited advice. Not about how to lead the tribe, or what I should do. It was about the one thing I shouldn't do.

I shouldn't get married.

"You absolutely cannot get married. You're supposed to lead us because the tribe needs you."

It was all they talked about. Nothing makes for a more awkward conversation than having zero marriage prospects and finding yourself in the middle of a tribe discussing it on social media. Pages upon pages of Facebook posts were dedicated to the topic.

It was surreal. I refused to address it. Privately, I kept saying that my getting married is none of anyone's business, but they just wouldn't budge. I understood, I suppose. The tribe could be led by an unmarried woman, apparently, as long as she was only defined as a *daughter of a tribal leader*. With marriage, I would be assigned my husband's status, not my father's anymore. It would create leadership problems for the tribe down the line. As if all of this wasn't complicated enough.

Although they were clearly making stuff up as they went, in the end I relented. I actually had to swear I wouldn't get married while I was leading the tribe, just to shut them all up. I found the entire proposition ridiculous. I didn't even know how I felt about marriage, yet here I was, fighting left and right over my nonexistent marriage prospects.

I finally set up a meeting with a couple of tribal elders. This time I was meeting them as a candidate. Surely, I thought, they'd finally see the light this time around and all this leadership business would go away. Like many other conversations with the tribal elders that I'd had over the years, this one also went in an entirely different direction than I expected.

Instead of objecting, they pledged their allegiance to me.

It was now a done deal, there was no getting out of it, so I started taking every meeting I could, trying to meet as many people as possible. For the first time, the new khan's audiences included the women. I kept going back and forth between Spin Boldak and Kandahar city, with poor Sangeena traveling with me as a chaperone. I kept receiving ambassadors from my community, until the district governor and every one of the leaders pledged their allegiance.

Things were moving so quickly, it wasn't until my very last meeting that I fully realized what I had taken on. I went to the house of the last tribal leader I was supposed to see. I still have the pictures from that day, although I don't really need them: the image is burned in my memory. I knew little about the leader that I was supposed to meet other than that he was my father's distant relative, and my father apparently helped him somehow back in the day. I never learned the full story.

It was not a very dignified visit. The drive was long. My sister's general lack of enthusiasm for her new role as my chaperone was on full display. She was spread out in the back seat, sleeping soundly. Thankfully, at least I was upright. The car window was open, and I was peeking out to see what was going on as the driver got out and knocked on the door. I could hear the driver say: "She's the daughter." Nothing else. There was no explanation of whose daughter, no other information was offered.

Before I could get out of the car, the old man walked up to me without a word. I just sat there not sure what to do as he studied my face through the window and then, to my shock, he started crying.

For a second, I thought it was because we looked so strange. In the corner of my eye I could see Sangeena shifting, unable to find a comfortable spot. I started shuffling too, unnerved by his crying. Outside of his title, I didn't even know who he was. I was only vaguely aware that he had history with my father, but not what it was. All I knew was that there was an old man crying at the sight of me. I couldn't make any sense of it.

When he finally spoke, he said, without ever introducing himself: "You're the one who is going to continue your father's work. You're going to make us proud, the way you always made him proud. You have to continue with whatever you are doing."

And then he said something I'll never forget: "You are him; you are him." I wasn't like him, I *was* him. The old man said it so forcefully, with such conviction. He equated me with someone I worshiped my entire life. It was the first time I realized that this was so much bigger than me.

Up until that point, I didn't really think about what the tribal leadership entailed beyond the logistics of it all. Up until then, it was just a mad rush to salvage my father's legacy and secure it for my brother. It was that old man crying in front of me that put it into perspective for the first time: I was now the tribe's champion. I was their hope. I was meant to protect them, the way my father protected them. The way my father protected *me*.

It was only his tears that made me realize that I, a twenty-three-year-old woman, was now the leader of one of Afghanistan's biggest, most influential tribes.

13

THE VERY BEGINNING OF MY KHANSHIP WAS NOT quite the raging success I had hoped for it to be. There was a knock on our door one night. A distraught man was asking if this was the house of Khan Pashtana. My brother, who opened the door, confirmed that it was. I was on the phone, arguing with someone, as one does, oblivious to my brother waving to get my attention.

My brother eventually realized trying to get me to come to the door was a losing battle and asked the man why he needed to see me. "My son is sick," the man explained. "He needs a doctor, and I don't have enough money to take him to see one. I asked my family, too, but no one had any money. I thought maybe my khan would help me."

My brother now started waving more forcefully until I muted my call, utterly annoyed, to hear what was going on. "Just give him the money!" I brushed my brother off. I registered through the corner of my eye that the man was thanking him through tears. I got off the phone, suddenly fully aware of how inappropriate my behavior was, wanting to fix it, wanting to talk to the man about his son. I wanted to tell him I'd pray for his child, but it was too late. The man already rushed off.

Way to go, I thought. My first request as a khan and I wasn't even gracious enough to listen to the man who came to me for help. I don't remember anymore who was on the phone, or why it seemed more important at the time to finish the conversation than to speak to the man with the dying son. I suspect I forgot because the reason wasn't nearly good enough. I'll learn, I promised myself. I'll learn.

The amount of attention that my position as the khan drew was another thing that took some getting used to. One time, as I was distributing food, an old man asked for my name as I handed him the package.

"Pashtana."

"No, no, your last name," he pressed.

"Durrani," I said, louder than intended, loud enough to announce it to the whole line. As soon as I said it, a younger man from the back of the line started running toward me. My brother, alarmed by the man's beeline, immediately puffed up his chest like a frog, getting ready to defend me. We both thought the man was about to attack me. Yelling as he ran toward me, it took a while to process what he was saying: "She's my khan, she's my khan!" I extended my arm across my brother's chest, just in case, to prevent him from punching the poor man. He just wanted to meet me. I am not sure if the man in his excitement ever realized how close he was to being pummeled.

With time though, it all settled into a routine.

I started dividing my time between Kabul and Kandahar: Kabul for studies and managing LEARN, and Kandahar for implementing projects and dealing with tribal affairs. I threw myself into work; being constantly busy distracted me from the weight of responsibility on my shoulders. Looking back, fitting in all my duties in a course of a day was a mathematical improbability, but I preferred it that way. Working quieted my mind, or at least silenced the chatter in my head.

By then, the entire country was already uneasy about the future. We'd been bracing ourselves for what was coming since February 2020, when the Taliban and the US reached the peace agreement.

The fact that there was no immediate reaction to the agreement was seen as a positive sign by the world, but the Afghans knew better: it was February, after all, and the Taliban were just hibernating. Winter repeatedly grinds everything to a halt in Afghanistan, and even fighting has to wait for March. As soon as the snow starts to melt, as soon as the flowers start blooming again, Taliban start dotting the scenery, accompanied by the fireworks of mortar launchers and crackling of gunfire. Fighting season would then rage from March to October, until it was once again beaten into submission by the harsh Afghan winter. Year after year, these spring offensives were the only thing that ran on time in the country, the one thing you could count on.

When we first started hearing that the US was holding face-to-face talks with the Taliban in 2018, the government vehemently opposed them. It was partially due to the fact that they weren't invited to attend: the negotiations took place without any Afghan government representatives. We may be the only country in which the government isn't invited to negotiate its own future, but then again, there are a lot of things in Afghanistan that are unimaginable anywhere else.

Instead of negotiating, the president busied himself contributing to Twitter campaigns about inalienable rights for women, the ones that the country wasn't willing to give up. While it was nice to read about Ghani having a red line, I really couldn't help but wonder why the head of a country was posting about human rights rather than making sure we had them.

When the Americans came to Afghanistan to fight the Taliban, it was the tribesmen who fought alongside the US special forces. Once the fighting was over, the tribesmen mostly outlived their usefulness in the eyes of the West. It was time to drag us into the twenty-first century, and they started looking for people a bit more like them, a bit more Afghan-ish than Afghan. Since Afghans have been contributing to the world's refugee population for several decades running, there was no shortage of those with dual citizenships. They were the ones tasked with straddling the cultural divide between the donors and the natives.

By the 2020s, that translated into us being ruled by the hyphenated Afghans: Afghan-Canadians, Afghan-Americans, Afghan-Germans. Being just Afghan didn't suffice, it needed to be fortified by the second country. It didn't matter all that much which one, as long as there was one.

Belonging is a strange thing. Being a refugee in Pakistan, not only was I not hyphenated, but in Kabul, it was often pointed out to me that I was not quite Afghan. You could only remain Afghan, it seemed, if you ran far enough; if you stopped too close, you didn't count at all. Adding insult to injury, actual Pakistanis were generally welcome. It was only Afghan refugees like me who were eyed with suspicion and considered less than.

Hyphenated Afghans were favored by the West, too, as leaders and partners, both within the government and the civil society. Afghanistan relied on handouts and the donors seemed relieved when someone spoke their language and understood their rules in this admittedly crazy country.

Although some of them promptly renounced their second citizenships as they entered politics, the hyphenated Afghans stuck together, as if sitting on two chairs automatically admitted you to a secret club and entitled you to a secret handshake. They patted each other on the back, picking and choosing which cultural norms to uphold based on their own interests. Ministries were overrun with them. They have never traveled in Afghanistan beyond Kabul, but the experience of having lived in the West replaced knowledge and expertise as a prerequisite for governance.

We all had our favorite official to complain about: the one promoted far out of their competency. Mine was the education minister who returned to Afghanistan following a career running a private school in Kabul. Nobody knows what she did in the US. Now, in Afghanistan, she sat on several committees, including Education and Women, and I was forced to deal with her on a regular basis. While most people knew better than to anger officials charged with approving their applications, I opposed mine publicly. When she proposed the idea of moving elementary education to the mosques, I wrote an open letter with a fellow Hazara activist, highlighting what a spectacularly bad idea that was. It not only excluded the girls and the minorities; the whole proposal was thin on common sense.

Clearly, she didn't forgive me for that open letter. She'd find a fault with every permit I applied for, every memorandum of understanding I submitted for her signature. One time she returned it because she didn't like the logo; another, because she objected to my use of Oxford commas. I suppose, as an American, she punctuated sparsely. I came out of a British system where the Oxford comma ruled supreme. The documents, with those inane comments about the size of the logo, or superfluous commas, would then come back to me, unsigned, delaying yet another project for months on end. We both knew that we had larger differences than just differing views on graphics and grammar.

United in their contempt for the tribes and tribal life, hyphenated Afghans failed to recognize that they now constituted a new tribe. After all, isn't associating yourself with people who share your background and values the very meaning of the word? They weren't there valiantly fighting tribalism as they claimed, they simply preferred their own tribe to the ones they found in Afghanistan. So, when the peace agreement excluded the government, it severed their kinship with the West. That's where the scaffolding started crumbling. That's when their tribe split.

The non-hyphenated part of the government was hardly any more relatable. The warlords constituted the second tier, occupying around half of all parliament seats from the very beginning. Initially they were from the cadre of mujahedeen who fought the Soviets, but later, there were newcomers, too—those whose fighting experience mainly consisted of providing muscle for the smuggling operations. The world at large didn't object to them too loudly, as long as they committed not to target the foreign troops. Representatives of the Afghan government only needed to commit to respecting the invading army's human rights—not ours. You see how that might become a problem down the line.

Despite everyone's best efforts, or more accurately, everyone's middling efforts, Afghanistan remained a place where human rights went to die.

Even when it came to the rights of women, the commitment was conditional, despite the relentless insistence that we should be prioritized. We were given the same constitutional rights, but subsequently the government kept adding laws that slowly chipped away at them, group by group, issue by issue. The law legalized marital rape. Child marriage became not only permissible again, but legal. Pushed into the gray areas of the law, for sure, but still there, still defensible.

Sometimes, the ironies were impossible to miss. As we read about the MeToo movement taking the world by storm, Afghanistan appointed a well-known serial rapist to the post of defense minister.

The government had little support, which was hardly surprising as they practically ran on a platform of not fully integrating. They still treated rural areas as nothing more than trading routes and sources of revenue, whether official or unofficial. With governing reduced to a financial transaction, the peace negotiations started looking more like a yard sale than a road to peace.

By the time the government finally joined the peace negotiations, there was little left to negotiate about. Corruption already choked us to death.

I was invited to participate in larger negotiations with the Taliban almost a year after the peace agreement, in February of 2021. It wasn't in my tribal role; there was no tribal representation at all on a political level. I was included as an education advocate. It was the civil society, a group that encompasses hundreds of NGOs operating in Afghanistan, that put my name forward as a representative. I was an odd choice, I suppose, despite my advocacy for girls' education. I was a token voice from the rural area, there in a sea of city girls. Mistrust, lack of understanding, and different realities kept colliding. I stubbornly kept wearing my tribal clothes to meetings, insisting that there's more to the future than looking the part. It sometimes seemed to me that the gap between urban and rural is even greater than the one between the Taliban and the government.

I understood well, both as an education advocate and as a

tribal leader, that the negotiations were necessary. I believed in engagement. I have openly and repeatedly criticized the government for not doing it sooner. We needed an inclusive government. We had to start making room for the opposing parties no matter what their stance might be. The Taliban were our reality, whether we liked it or not, as they have been for the past twenty-five years. Trying to wish them away didn't constitute a strategy. Peace talks were meant to ensure that they don't become our *sole* reality. This perpetual time travel we faced, further and further into the past, could have been prevented by inclusion, by power sharing. The Taliban never opened a single school in the areas they controlled in the past two decades or in the areas they took over during the siege. The Taliban kept making fake promises and journalists in the West believed them. There were articles written that showed the Taliban as tolerant. But all they were tolerant towards was their own daughters' education, not the education of Afghan girls. It seemed like the West was conspiring against the women of Afghanistan. There were op-eds published in major newspapers in the U.S. that whitewashed the Taliban. Deep inside, I knew it was easier to believe we could live on Mars than to think that the Taliban had changed.

Yet for all my insistence on negotiations, when it came to personal involvement, I had nothing but reservations. Engaging personally with the group my father fought against, in any form, even if it were on the periphery, felt like a betrayal. Maybe, had he been alive, had I had his counsel, I wouldn't have struggled as much. My father would have advocated pragmatism, I knew; he would have insisted it was the best for our community. But he wasn't there, and I had to live with the fact that my first consequential political decision went against everything he stood for.

Talking to my tribe, talking to the girls, somewhat assuaged the sense of guilt that I felt for participating. Most people in the province, even the women, wanted the Taliban in the government.

The tribe I represented lost some 2,300 men in this fight. It's a small district, not very densely populated, and year after year, they'd wrap their sons in white burial cloths and lay them into the ground. The only statistic worse than our literacy rates was our death toll.

Now they wanted the fight to end. For them, the discussion wasn't about the quality of life. The issue was survival. My political preferences, I realized, were a sign of my privilege. They just wanted to live.

Although negotiating hadn't done a whole lot of good in the past, wasn't it time to try in earnest? Even I thought that perhaps folding the Taliban into politics would soften their most extreme views; after all, all those warlords admitted to the parliament calmed down once they were folded into the government. There were fewer massacres, fewer warlord-initiated military campaigns, the death count was lower. Power sharing could temper the Taliban, too.

My country is a large dysfunctional family, and every day is like sitting down for an uncomfortable, never-ending Thanksgiving dinner that inevitably ends up in a shoot-out. I thought if we kept talking, the guns wouldn't come out so quickly. Because if it came to that, we all knew that both sides were willing to die for it.

Every time the Taliban took over my heart sank. I knew it was over for that area when it came to constitutional rights or just the right to exist. When the Taliban took over Kandahar, they asked women to leave their banking jobs and send their brothers to replace them. I cried my eyes out, mourning the ambitious Afghan daughters who could have been the saviors of our war-torn country.

For all their chest thumping, the Taliban were as much of an import as the Western concept of democracy they fought against.

The Deobandi movement started in India in the nineteenth century as a result of India's struggle for independence from the British. The Deobandis believed that a return to pure, strict Islam would enable them to overthrow the occupation. After the independence and the partition of India, Deobandi madrassas spread around the region, but the Pakistani-Afghan border seemed to contain most of them. To truly take root, the movement needed an external enemy, and the Soviet invasion readily provided one. The philosophy resonated with the refugee boys who ended up in those madrassas. In an abundance of irony given their stance on education, they called themselves Talibs, or "students." Armed with Deobandi beliefs and American weapons, they went to fight, as individuals, not as a group yet, and the ideology fused with Wahabism, brought by so many foreigners who came to fight against the Soviets. They too mixed and matched their beliefs, creating a strand of political Islam that was unique to the Taliban. Pakistan, first under Zia and then under Benazir Bhutto, watched and cheered them on.

Once the Soviets retreated, there was an all-out war between the various mujahedeen groups. The Taliban entered Afghanistan as a militia, fighting the warlords in post-Soviet Afghanistan. They initially received community support as a party of law and order in a country that had neither. They grew stronger, joined by some twenty thousand students from Pakistani madrassas, the religious schools.

So you see, even the Taliban is a product of their education.

They were refugees, like me.

They were mostly Pashtuns, like me.

Like me, they first saw their home country in their teens.

Except for the education—and gender—we weren't that different. Just remember that next time you're tempted to say that education should wait until you're done fighting wars and building infrastructure.

Within two years of being formed, the Taliban took Kabul and officially started their reign. The takeover was brutal in the extreme: Dr. Najib, Afghanistan's former president, was abducted from the UN compound, tortured, and killed. They dragged his body through Kabul before finally hanging him on an electricity pole. Women of all ethnicities and tribal affiliations disappeared from the public eye, denied access to education or employment, required to cover up and shut up, denied existence in the public space without a male guardian.

Now the Taliban was saying they were willing to compromise if they were included in the government. True, they kept fighting the same government they were supposed to negotiate with, but no one found it strange. There was going to be one more set of negotiations, this time with the Afghan government included, and the Taliban needed to negotiate from the position of strength. It's simple math: the more territory you hold, the stronger the negotiating position. But the speed at which they were acquiring territory gave everyone pause. They were now going in leaps and bounds. The peace deal, the announced departure of US troops, emboldened them. The Taliban didn't think twice before slaughtering anyone who had been a civil servant or part of the government. The negotiations were a sham and the Taliban played both parties: the US that lied when they said they stood for human rights and the Afghan government that was delusional, thinking somebody was going to come to save them. The provincial governments fought as much as they could while the Kabul elites partied. The national army was abandoned. They were left to fight for days without any supplies. Horrific videos of the Taliban murdering army personnel came out of those fighting zones.

In July, the Taliban controlled the border crossings with Pakistan, Tajikistan and Iran, with the Taliban flag flying over them. Looking at those flags, all I could think about were my father's stories growing up. The stories of them taking the country away from the Taliban. The stories of resistance, of building the country from the ground up.

"We gathered just outside Kandahar, waiting for Karzai," my father had told us. Karzai would later become the first democratically elected president of Afghanistan. "But when he finally landed on the patch of grass before us, none of us paid attention to him. We just kept looking at the helicopter! We had never seen anything like it. It was black and so big that we wondered how it managed to fly at all. The night didn't seem dark at all. The whole valley was lit by the moon. It was so bright you could mistake it for daylight."

He said all the tribal leaders hugged him and kissed him on the hand, pledging their allegiance to them.

As a child, I'd go through my father's things, through his memory box, looking for a treasure. Instead of yelling at me for rummaging through his personal belongings without permission, he'd help me pull them out, one by one, explaining why he kept them.

One of them was an old flag, which he first hung in his office in Spin Boldak, which he saved and stored when it became too frayed to officially use.

"Tell the flag story, tell the flag story," I would always beg.

It was his favorite, too.

Replacing the white Taliban flag with the Afghan tricolor was their first victory in 2001. My father was there as they pulled the tricolor up the pole at the border crossing.

Afghanistan changed flags often, but the three colors persisted, since the inception of modern Afghanistan.

Each color on the flag was a symbol: the black stood for the troubles behind us, the red was for the blood spilled to obtain our freedom, and the green was the symbol of the better future. Those were the colors that we kept dressing all of our refugee children in. You cannot grow up in a refugee camp without having at least once in your life owned a tri-color outfit. Those colors remained when there was nothing else left of our country.

My father talked about being there as the Afghan flag was raised again as a pivotal moment, as his contribution to Afghan history. So, when on July 14, 2021, the white Taliban flag replaced the tricolor in Spin Boldak, my heart broke. It was my father who put the tricolor there.

It's just a flag, I kept trying to convince myself; the country wasn't lost yet. Deep down, however, I knew that this was the day my father's Afghanistan was gone.

What I mourned was not the government. I mourned the loss of color on our flag, the loss of color in our lives. I mourned the loss of the constitution, the one thing that gave me a voice as a woman in the country I loved with all my heart.

14

The countryside lit up with fighting, rolling down the hills like fireworks. One by one, villages started falling, until the Taliban reached the outskirts of Kandahar.

Recognizing the pattern of loss was part of my education; it was my very first lecture on my very first trip to Afghanistan: "For three hundred years, whoever takes Kandahar, takes the country. And in order to take Kandahar, you have to take the prison."

If there was anything I knew, it was my country's history. Yet, despite my fluency in reading the tea leaves of impending doom, it was hard for me to see how any of it was applicable to me.

Maybe we all live through history unaware.

We learn it, the way you learn the rules of cricket, but then when you watch the game for the first time, the rules haven't been internalized yet. For all your theory, it just looks like a bunch of men standing around, occasionally hurling a ball. Collectively, we all understand the theory of loss. It just never pierces the armor of hope. One day, someone will be pardoned. One day, someone will be the first one to escape the inevitable. For all you know, it could be you.

Maybe that's the reason most people flee so late. It's not that they don't know what's going to happen, especially not in Afghanistan where fleeing should be an Olympic discipline. It's part hope, part disbelief that keeps you put. You still think you're on the outside of it all.

So, like everyone else in Kandahar, I watched the fireworks, listened to the explosions, and waited, hoping that the history would bypass me, that I would be spared.

Firmly and comfortably ensconced in my denial, I ignored the implications when a friend, living on the prison side of town, asked me to take his mother and sisters in. "But of course they can stay with us. We'd be happy to have them." By the end of that week, almost every home in Kandahar housed internally displaced people. The Taliban were now coming from the prison side. They were on the path taken by every invading army.

Still, we waited.

Slowly, women disappeared from the street. There was no more shopping for groceries, no more everyday chores. That absence of life, absence of noise was eerie. It took me one video to realize that the Taliban didn't need to do much to silence me. All they needed to do was blackmail me like they did to Fatima Rahmati, an activist whose brothers were taken; she was forced to reverse her statements on civil rights in order to save them. The only things

I had were my pride and honor. I would lose them if I was forced to make a statement in the Taliban's favor. I thought of all those women who had to give up their freedom because they were worried about their family, who had to choose between freedom and family. That thought broke me.

With women locked up all around the province, the men went out to fight. Not the Taliban, but each other: whoever had an old score to settle was now out with a gun, breaking down the doors of his enemies. Still angry about someone's comment from fifteen years ago? This was your time to get even.

The lawlessness that precedes the takeover, that window of opportunity when the old authority is on its way out and the new one is yet to arrive, is the golden age of violence. It felt less like living history and more like watching a season finale of *Sons of Anarchy*. Almost a thousand were killed in infighting before the Taliban was anywhere near being in control of the province. None of it seemed real until the burials started.

It was only when the bloodletting was over that people started fleeing en masse. Despite the fact that most provincial capitals were now in Taliban hands, that the sea of humanity was flowing toward Kabul, the government didn't think about setting up the tents for the internally displaced, or about providing food for them and securing medicine and sanitation. They, too, remained true to themselves: they were busy preparing for the feeding frenzy that was about to commence.

Along the way, the army that still hadn't received any support from the government, neither salaries nor food, continued to lay down their weapons, in district after district. "Why aren't we resisting? Where is our air force?" we all wondered out loud.

It was not a rhetorical question.

Despite all the evidence of corruption in all other sectors, we still hoped the army could be that one exception that proved the rule. Surely they wouldn't steal the money earmarked for the army? Weren't they the ones defending not only us, but the government?

As devastating, as humiliating as it was to watch the country slowly fold, I understood the lack of resistance too. How many sons are you meant to sacrifice to a government that doesn't care, that doesn't fix, that requires more and more blood to be spilled without giving anything in return?

There came a night when we knew with certainty that the fall of Kandahar was inevitable, although maybe not yet imminent. We just knew the course changed irrevocably. I don't know what changed, or how we knew. The pressure gauge rose steadily until it hit red. We could all hear the sound, clearly. The air smelled different.

I needed to get my family out. I needed them to be safe, and for them, Pakistan was the only place that offered safety.

I refused to leave with them, though.

I had to stay because I had a seminar that was to take place in Kandahar in three weeks. I was sitting on some three hundred tablets, the largest shipment so far. I was supposed to distribute them there. We booked a hotel conference room for the seminar. We booked a photographer. I had the totes ready for the girls. I had to stay here.

"The conference room is already paid for," I kept telling my mother, as if that explained anything at all. "You should leave. I will do what I have to do and then go to Kabul to wait it out." I needed to go to Kabul anyway to secure the last permit for the new community school. "Things will calm down," I assured her.

There was little for me in Pakistan. Pakistan has a limited supply of tolerance for opinions like mine. Political differences, the ones that in other countries get resolved through political means, can quickly turn fatal in our part of the world. Shutting up after all this time just didn't seem like an option. If it comes to that, if that was the price to pay, I'd rather be silenced in Afghanistan.

As long as I didn't leave the country, I wasn't giving up, I thought to myself. There was little I could do for my tribe, but I still had LEARN, my staff, and my girls to worry about. I was one stamp short of a government approval for the community school. The education minister would definitely stamp it now that all of us were running out of time.

Yes, that was the best plan, I decided. My family needed to leave and I'd go to Kabul after they left, where I could still deal with LEARN, still deal with tribal issues.

My mother was apoplectic. She kept pointing out the utter stupidity of my plan, my refusal to accept the reality. "The car is ready! There is nowhere to go but Pakistan! You won't make it to Kabul! They'll close the airport! How do you think you'll get there?"

Her arguments would have been far more convincing had she not been clutching a little plastic bag she prepared for her trip to Pakistan. It held enough clothes to last her a week. For generations we fled with a few plastic bags, lying to ourselves that it was all temporary. I dug my heels in. We were at an impasse. When she couldn't talk sense into me, she yelled at me in frustration.

By the time they left, we exchanged a fair share of harsh words.

This could have been our last conversation, we both knew it, yet we both stubbornly persisted in yelling. It damages your soul, but you don't see it in the heat of the argument. I hugged my siblings through tears, but my mother left unhugged, slamming the door behind her, with me still listing my reasons for staying. It was only once the door closed behind them that both of us regretted it. The words, at least, if not actions: we were both doing what we thought was necessary.

My mother called in the morning, as soon as she arrived at

her sister's house. Our own house in Quetta was now out of reach, with my uncles all settled there with a door bolted to keep us out. My mother cried and said she was sorry, and then I cried and said I was sorry.

She was right, I admitted, I was stuck in Kandahar, unable to go to Kabul, as if proving her right would offer her relief.

To the surprise of no one at all, the Kandahar Airport closed that night because of the fighting. It would take days to reopen, and even then, the flights were full, and tickets were impossible to come by. Driving to Kabul was out of the question, even if I were willing to consider it as an option, which I wasn't. My father always insisted that driving from Kandahar to Kabul wasn't safe, even at the best of times, let alone now.

I felt alone without my family around me, but I was glad they were gone, glad they were safely out. One thing less to worry about. It felt like such a selfish thought, but my mind played it on a loop.

It took another three days to get on a flight to Kabul. I was manic. You could already feel the Taliban presence in the city. The city wasn't theirs yet, but you could tell they were getting ready to pounce. I needed to get out until the takeover was final, until it settled.

Takeovers should be avoided at all cost. That's the time when none of the rules apply. All it takes is one angry man with a gun. That's the time of ultimate uncertainty, that one time when it's impossible to talk your way out, because no one stops to listen.

When I finally got the plane ticket to Kabul, I promised myself I'd return to Kandahar as soon as things calmed down. Even with the Taliban in charge in the province, as long as there's power sharing, there was hope. All I needed to do was wait in Kabul for a bit until the dust settled.

As soon as I arrived in Kabul, I set in motion plans to evacuate my staff. We were on the official list of protected NGOs, like some endangered wildlife facing extinction. Western countries were feverishly expatriating their Afghan allies: from the special forces trained by the Americans, to the NGOs that advocated ideas like education that could easily mean a death sentence under the Taliban. I'd get calls advising me to leave, but instead of complying, I just kept adding names of my staff to their list. I didn't listen to my mother when she ordered me to leave; the State Department stood no chance at all. I needed to ensure that LEARN continued to exist, though, regardless of how unbearable I may find the idea of separating the work from the girls.

Then, I set off to get the final government signoff for a community school I was planning to open. The ministries were still operating as usual, in every sense of the word: the education minister refused to sign off on my project. I never felt more defeated. The country was burning, but the government kept playing the fiddle.

I also needed to register with my negotiating group for the peace talks. They needed my passport to put me on the list of negotiators. It seems so ridiculous in retrospect—what negotiations? Was I blind? But dutifully, I handed over my passport. There was nothing else left for me to do in Kabul and I started thinking about going back to Kandahar. The situation there didn't seem that dire from afar. Failing to address the bigger picture is something of a trait of mine, I now realize. I wanted to prepare for the seminar. The totes we'd give out at the end of it wouldn't be empty this time. There would be a tablet inside each one. I waited for years to fill those totes for them. This was going to be a big moment for me and my girls.

I watched as the news shows painted the maps red signifying Taliban advances. I knew that every stroke of that brush would obscure the faces of women, until they disappear, until their voices aren't heard again. There were desperate posts on social media from educated women, pledging publicly to be good, hard-working, loyal citizens in whichever country takes them. It was heartbreaking, but I kept thinking of the women of Kandahar Province. They couldn't even post their misery. Over half of them are illiterate. They'll perish in silence behind closed doors, the way they lived. It will be like they never really existed. *I am a Kandahari woman.* What am I doing here in Kabul, away from my girls, away from my tribe?

I wanted to be with them for the last chapter that mentions us. Pay a debt to my father, my family, my girls. I wanted to be home. Home is the site of all of our unimaginable losses.

15

FLEW BACK TO KANDAHAR A FEW DAYS BEFORE THE
city fell. As I landed, the prison was overrun.
The entire population was running north, toward Kabul, and I decided to go in the other
direction. It was like running back into a house
on fire, pointless to anyone except for the person
needing to say goodbye.

I knew I may have to leave in the end, but
isn't coming in last what we expect of all our
women? We feed them last, we educate them
last. Well then, I'll join the end of the line. I'll
be the last to leave.

I couldn't reach any of my students. The idea
of a seminar, for which I came back, was laugh-

able. The sense of loss was so enormous, so overwhelming, I was hollowed out. Nothing could fill the void.

I got interview requests for that night: girl education advocate in Kandahar as the city is falling? Party of one.

The interview was with Channel Four, a British TV network. They reached out on Twitter, or maybe Instagram; I was apparently the last fool in Kandahar to post rather than pack.

Would I talk to them?

Sure I would.

On the phone, they kept suggesting, citing safety concerns.

No, I insisted. Zoom, in full view.

If this was to be the last time I got to show my face, I might as well do it on TV.

"Are you sure?"

I have rarely been more certain of anything in my life.

It felt like I was tasked with reading a eulogy, and you don't obscure your face when you read a eulogy. Kandahar deserved better than that.

We all deserved better than that.

I never watched the interview, and I don't remember it all that clearly, but I've heard enough about it to be able to picture it.

It was strange to be asked on live television about dying.

What would you do if they come knocking?

"Pray," I responded. "I'd pray." What else is there to do but to make peace with God when I couldn't get it anywhere else?

They asked about my girls, and for a moment, my eyes filled with tears. Not enough to have to wipe them, I certainly don't remember wiping them. I collected myself and answered their question.

Once the interview was over, my Twitter exploded.

A few messages expressed pride that there was someone from Kandahar speaking up. The rest of them, however, debated my apparent lack of courage. The fact that I teared up. Saying I should have been braver; how I shouldn't have cried in public. God forbid we show emotion. You haven't seen a stiff upper lip until you've been to Afghanistan.

I didn't have the energy to react. I wasn't an eighteen-year-old who just survived a bomb attack and was facing a backlash for trying to save a man. I didn't need to prove anything to anyone. Was there nothing better out there to discuss when the world was crumbling around us other than whether a woman should cry at the sight of it? Had we resisted the Taliban as valiantly as we resist showing emotion I wouldn't be packing now. I had enough of being judged.

This time, even I knew this was a goodbye. The go sign is the sharp pain in your chest that's impossible to ease. Your chest only expands to the smallest of breaths, your breathing becomes labored. That's when you know that all is lost. It's like being underwater and running out of breath. You can come up for air or just drown. Unexpectedly, you learn it's a decision to make, not an instinct to follow.

No one teaches you how to pack when you're about to leave your life behind. I kept putting things in the bag, then taking them out. Some things were not up for debate: I packed the prayer beads my father left me, and his tribal ring made of lapis lazuli, a blue rock of Afghanistan that has been mined for six thousand years. It stands for royalty and honor and truth. It stands for my father and my tribe.

I packed a miniature Quran, my father's favorite, a gift from my mother years ago. I packed his treasure box. Those were the things that went in first.

I packed a book I was reading. Sarah gave it to me almost a year ago, and I was still on page 378—it was a busy year. I hate leaving books unfinished. I packed it, rationalizing the space it took by saying that there was no guarantee that I'd be able to afford to buy it once I leave. It was Samantha Power's *The Education of an Idealist*. I was too upset to notice the irony at the time.

I took my jewelry with me. Jewelry has nothing to do with adorning yourself. For Afghan women, it's a security bond meant to present as money when it's needed.

I scoffed at having to take clothes, choosing only a few pieces that were hand embroidered by the old women from my tribe.

My cousin sent his car and his driver to get me out of the city; only people who worked for the family for decades were to be trusted. You could only trust your tribe. I left at dawn, and the road out of Kandahar city was empty. I expected it to be dotted with people, looking like a funeral procession, but everybody was locked up in their homes, hiding. I did as I promised; I was the last to leave.

I traveled alone, marred by guilt at leaving my girls behind, down the same road I took when I entered Afghanistan for the first time.

I felt the presence of all those who fled before me, a long line of refugees weighing the earth down. The weight is not from what they carry: few manage to bring anything of use with them. Especially us latecomers, the ones that already waited too long. We travel light. The heaviness comes from pressing the earth underneath us with the full weight of our loss. Loss of dignity, of people, possessions, a future. We keep losing on repeat.

It's the same road my father took to fight the Taliban, the same one he traveled down to be buried. The road that splits all our lives in two. The road of "before" and "after." The road that is now slowly stripping me of everything: my tribe, my khanship, my rights.

The road that reminds you that our choices have always been between the lesser of two evils; they were never about hope.

As I leave, all I can think of is seeing Afghanistan for the first time. I remember my shock at seeing the sea of blue. I hear my father in my head, over and over saying: "You have to learn to look past the burqas." With Kandahar city disappearing behind me, I keep the conversation going; dead or alive, my father is still the person I turn to in moments of greatest joy and greatest despair. "Maybe it's not as trivial, Father. Maybe we shouldn't look past them. It's been almost a hundred years since Afghan women got their right to vote; it's been almost a hundred years since Queen Soraya ripped a veil off her face in protest. And look at them, Father, they're drawing a curtain on us again."

Burqas do matter, Father. I should know. Because as I was leaving Kandahar behind, I was wearing one.

16

ALL IT TOOK WAS TEN DAYS. BY AUGUST 15, THE entire country was gone. The Taliban entered Kabul and vowed to restore law and order, but few felt reassured. Within days, the Ministry for Women's Affairs was turned into a Ministry of Vice and Virtue. Time is circular in Afghanistan.

Masses of people were on the move, trying to outrun their fate. Tribal regions were swelling with the displaced. Those who weren't running watched in disbelief, live on television, as the triumphant Taliban held their first press conference from the presidential palace. Like most Afghans, I hadn't slept for days. Since I fled Kandahar, losses kept rolling in until there was nothing left to lose.

Images from the airport looked like they ought to be seen in black and white, like a history lesson from a different century. On the borders, people were packed in the narrow strip of no-man's-land so tightly that if you'd dropped a coin, it could never reach the ground. They were kept back by the fence that's topped with the concertina wire like some intricate icing on a metal cake; their lives suspended, their gazes empty. The rug was pulled out from underneath us, and we collectively lost our balance. The fall, however, seemed to be from a much greater height. We were sold out.

The Taliban announced amnesty, but no one was willing to stake their lives on Taliban's better nature prevailing. The desperation was palpable, visible to the naked eye. A man fell to his death trying to hold on to a wheel on the plane that was taking off without him. Everyone I knew was trying to secure humanitarian parole, that entry to the brave new world, where at least your survival is guaranteed.

When I finally joined my family in Pakistan, they were in Quetta, staying with my mother's relatives. There was nowhere else for them to go: our own house in Quetta, the house where my siblings and I grew up, was now occupied by my uncle's family. When he claimed it as his own after my father's death, no one really mourned the loss of it. Back then, him taking it only provoked anger. Now, this act rendered us homeless.

Despite all that, my family lived in relative peace until I joined them. Afghanistan was still in the news, and I was still getting interview requests from all over the world. From my relatives' basement I continued speaking out, challenging the Taliban and criticizing Pakistan's treatment of refugees. Although my mother's family was no more enamored with my activism than the relatives on my father's side, they graciously allowed it. I wouldn't disclose my location in interviews, even though I was now in Pakistan. It was a flimsy effort to protect the people who gave us a refuge from the wrath of those who insisted I should shut up once and for all. It wasn't enough. Some helpful soul doxed me and published the address of the house on social media, an open invitation for a riot. We left the same day for Karachi, some eight hours away, thinking it would be easier to disappear there. We reasoned that Karachi has a population of almost 15 million, so it would be like looking for a needle in a haystack. Still, I promised, no more interviews from there.

I knew Karachi was a temporary measure. My family needed to be in Quetta, where my mother had the support of her family. As for me, Pakistan as a whole was hardly an option. I could never run LEARN from there.

Evacuations in Afghanistan were still ongoing, and there was a list of people who were eligible for it. I was on it. The top of the list was reserved for those who cooperated with NATO in any way. The second tier consisted of NGOs. Among the NGOs, the most vulnerable ones were those who advocated for women and for education, given the Taliban's stance on those issues. As the head of LEARN, I managed to combine the two of the Taliban's least favorite things into a single NGO. I ticked all the boxes. If this were a climate change disaster, I'd be a polar bear on a melting ice cap.

I kept getting messages from the evacuation coordinators to go to Kabul Airport to be evacuated. "I'm in Karachi! In Pakistan! Wrong country, AND I'm five hundred kilometers away!"

It wasn't just the distance, though. I naively thought that I didn't need a parole. I had a US visitor visa. It seemed like a lifetime ago, but LEARN was featured in a documentary, and I was invited to an event in New York to promote it. The visa was approved weeks ago. All they needed to do was stamp it into my passport. "Can't I just use that? I'd look for a university to take me once I'm there."

I reached out to everyone I knew, but most were incredulous.

"You're approved for a humanitarian parole, but you want a visitor visa? What, you want to be a tourist, when the rest of the country is trying to run for their lives?"

I tried to explain that I, too, was trying to run for my life; I was just trying to take a different route. The one that didn't require me giving up my country in the process. I have exhausted myself trying to prove I'm a true Afghan. I wasn't going to be chased out. Who gets to be an Afghan if we all give up on Afghanistan? I was both offended and chastened by their reference to tourism. "I'm looking for a university that will take me in once I'm there," I kept repeating. It didn't help. I was told I was creating unnecessary problems. Once or twice, people hinted I was being ungrateful.

I probably was. But I just couldn't let go. I was born a refugee. I went back by myself to that godforsaken country because it was home. Now, along with millions of other Afghans, I was losing it yet again. I refused to believe that my Afghan passport, the one I was so proud of, was good only for stamping a refugee visa in. I was tired of being exiled. I wasn't going to give up my citizenship, and that was the end of that.

Jess was the first to crack.

I met Jess in summer of 2021. She contacted me, out of the blue; she ran her own NGO, negotiating satellite services for educational purposes, and she wondered if I would be interested in participating in it. Would I ever.

Jess was also a major in the US Army. Last deployed to Afghanistan in 2013, she was part of the group of US Army Special Ops who trained the first female members of Afghan special forces. Now she was knee-deep in the unofficial evacuation effort, tracking her fellow Afghan women soldiers down to whatever provinces they were last seen fighting in, trying to get them to Kabul and out of the country. She was the keeper of the Schindler's list. Although not even she could pull off a tourist visa, she at least understood my stubborn desire to keep my ties to my country. After all, she was willing to die for hers.

Jess introduced me to Amna, a journalist originally from Pakistan. "She may be able to help." Amna had strong ties with Wellesley College. "You'd be a perfect fit there. It's an all-women's college; they have a research institute that may be interested in offering you a fellowship so you could continue working on LEARN." I nodded, wondering why Amna thought I was the one that needed convincing.

Amna made good on her word. I still don't know how she managed to pull it off, but within a couple of weeks, I received an email that offered me a two-year fellowship at Wellesley's Centers for Women. Most important, the email included the magic words: "We will take care of your visa."

In my fight to secure a visa that was to my liking, I overlooked a minor detail.

I didn't have an actual passport to stamp it in.

In my infinite wisdom, back in July, I left my passport in Kabul. Back when I was asked to participate in the negotiations with the Taliban, I submitted it to the NGO that was heading the delegation so they could process me.

I wasn't even sure how to start looking for it. Since Kabul fell in August, the entire NGO world was on the run. When I finally tracked down the man to whom I handed over my passport, I realized in horror that he was on his way to France. "Don't worry, I left your passport in the office," he tried to reassure me. "It's the second drawer on the left. It should be easy to get it."

I listened to him in disbelief. Although I was the idiot who left her passport in Kabul, I wasn't able to curb my sarcasm: "Yes, easy. I need to organize a burglary, and then the relay race from Kabul to Quetta, dodging the Taliban along the way."

In the end, however, that was exactly what I did. I was able to rely on my employees, friends, and tribesmen to get it from Kabul to Kandahar, but no one was willing to get it across the border. Not until my sister volunteered to do it.

My siblings and I perpetually seem like we're on the verge of killing each other. Within the walls of the house, insults fly; we snap at each other, call each other names. I've been calling both my brother and my sister "donkey" for so long that they started responding to it. Yet whatever differences there may be, I knew there was nothing we wouldn't do for each other.

I was both grateful and terrified at the prospect of Sangeena going. Rationally, I understood that this was the only way: she crossed legally, back in July, and could, in theory at least, come and go as she pleased. But crossing the border wasn't really a problem—I was the living proof of it. The problem was Kandahar. There were active searches, house to house. All tribal leaders were still in hiding. Our house in Kandahar was already ransacked; our tribe had lost all its influence under the new Taliban regime. I knew that me being in Kandahar would require more protection than they could give. Sangeena, on the other hand, never publicly criticized anyone, so she was less of a target. In Kandahar, she would be just another woman in a burqa.

I was flooded with guilt, but now was not the time to voice my thoughts. I kept hurling all the usual insults her way, hoping to ward off evil. My mother was well past burning sage for protection and had now progressed to sacrificing goats to ensure our safety. Sangeena going in to get my passport was about to get the second goat killed. My mother—or the goats—didn't know it yet, but it would take four goats for me to get out.

Bundled up in a burqa, Donkey headed to Kandahar city accompanied by a relative. I didn't take a full breath until she got back into Pakistan, but she managed to smuggle my passport across the border—in her bra.

There was no time to exhale. As soon as she handed me the passport, I took it to the US Consulate to get the visa stamped in it. That was it. I had already handed over the daily grind of the tribal leadership to my brother, who finally turned eighteen. I never really unpacked my bags, so there was nothing else I needed to do. My flight to Boston was the following day. I had a two-year fellowship to work on LEARN. Wellesley College was waiting for me.

The US Consulate staff offered to accompany me to the airport, to smooth any possible issues with the Pakistani border control. I said goodbye to my mother, to my brother, and my sister, but was still unable to take in fully what was happening as I arrived at the airport.

It took almost four hours before the consular staff admitted defeat. The Pakistanis refused to let me out. They helpfully explained that since I don't have the entry stamp for Pakistan, they couldn't possibly give me the exit one. No amount of talking was going to change that.

I went back to the house, back to my family, with all my luggage, devastated. "We'll try again, one more time, tomorrow. It will be different people at the airport, and they'll send a higher-ranking official with me this time. Surely this time it will work." I wanted to believe, but my mother looked unconvinced.

The following evening, I said my goodbyes yet again, we all cried some more, and I got into the car.

Six hours later, having failed to get on the plane once again, we left the airport. The vice consul looked defeated as he got in the car. "It's best if you don't go back home for a while. Stay at the consulate for a day or two." I finally broke down. I sobbed and sobbed the entire way to the consulate. I sobbed as they opened the gate of the consulate, I sobbed as they took my luggage in, and I sobbed as they closed the door behind me. I had the golden ticket, the visa that people were willing to die for, and I wasn't able to leave Pakistan, the country that didn't want me to begin with.

By now, even those around me were getting angry at the situation. It was a welcome change, as their anger was normally directed at me. It all seemed petty and unnecessary. Everyone I knew mobilized to help, my friends, my family.

"If you get registered in Pakistan as a refugee, they would have no reason to deny you," someone suggested.

Strings were pulled, documents were submitted.

It felt like I was on the outside of my body for days. When I got home to my mother, I sat at the dinner table, neither talking nor eating, responding only if my name was called out three times, like Voldemort. It was almost 11:00 p.m. when I got another text from one of the evacuation coordinators, politely enquiring about my ETA at the Kabul Airport. I wasn't sure if I should laugh or cry, and just stared at the phone for a while. Then I said, to no one in particular: "He's right. What am I doing here in Pakistan? They'll never let me leave. I might as well go back." My mother's relief that I was talking again was quickly tempered by the words I was saying.

"I need to be evacuated from Afghanistan. If I fly from there, they couldn't turn me around. I should try to go to Kabul."

My mother cleared the table without saying a word.

It spiraled from there. *In for a penny, in for a pound*, I thought. If I'm going to risk my life going to Afghanistan anyway, I could also finish a few things while there. I had the tablets; I could distribute them. I didn't require the ministry's approval anymore because there was no ministry. I could open that last community school. I could round the girls up, get it all going. And then, after I set up the school, the tribesmen would help get me to Kabul. The idea of going to Kabul suddenly didn't sound crazy at all. That evacuation coordinator who kept texting me wasn't uninformed, he was prescient.

It took a couple of weeks to set up the trip, because I kept adding things to do and places to visit. The plan slowly evolved from going from Quetta to Kabul Airport to be evacuated, to me touring Afghanistan. I'd stop in Kandahar city first, I decided. I had started a maternal healthcare program in the province before Afghanistan fell and I needed to make sure that the ultrasound machines had been delivered to the clinics that we'd set up. With the Taliban in charge, women couldn't get out easily anymore, and mobile clinics were the way to ensure they didn't have to travel too far. I started a blitz campaign to secure the money for the machines.

When Sangeena announced that she'd go back with me, my mother just threw her arms up in the air; there was nothing left to say. One stupid decision after another rendered her speechless. Her children were idiots. She was done with us. There were not enough goats in the world to keep us alive.

Donkey and I headed to the border together, just as we did all those years ago when our father took us to Afghanistan for the first time. This time, crossing held no joy; it felt oppressive, it sucked the air out of our lungs. A friend greeted us on the other side and took us farther into the province.

Once I was back in Afghanistan, I felt like myself again. I met with the girls, I got the school going, I taught a few classes, too. I immediately started wondering if I should just try to stay. Could I continue living like this, moving from one house to another? Not a single person thought it would be a good idea, but I kept talking about it until a friend of my father's shut me up once and for all. "You can do so much more for them on the outside. You have a network in place already, rely on it. In a few months, when everybody forgets about Afghanistan, you'll be out there to remind them."

I knew he was right. Grudgingly, I admitted it was time to leave.

COVID-19 WAS STILL A CONCERN IN OCTOBER OF 2021, AND IN ORDER to get on a plane, I needed to get vaccinated and then tested before the flight. The vaccine part was easy: the maternal healthcare program gave me enough allies who could smuggle me into the Kandahar hospital and give me the vaccine without entering me into the system that the Taliban now had access to. They managed to secure the single shot vaccine too, although I'd half hoped they wouldn't. Waiting for a second shot would allow me to stay in Afghanistan several weeks longer. The test, however, needed to be done at the clinic. There would be no special arrangements. I'd have to walk into a hospital full of Taliban fighters. "It will be a good practice for Kabul," I tried to reassure everyone around me. But of course I was apprehensive: the swab, taken from your nose, required me to uncover, to show my face. The same face I so cleverly insisted on showing on numerous TV networks complaining about the Taliban.

Right across from the testing station there was an OB-GYN office, because what better place to test people for a highly infectious disease than at the feet of the pregnant women. As I waited in the corner, there was a Talib sitting in one of the chairs outside the OB-GYN's office, waiting for his wife to come out. His daughter was running around, causing commotion, but he just smiled and offered her a spot on his knee. She gladly hopped on. I watched in disbelief. He clearly loved his daughter. I couldn't understand. Why choose to join a fight that would deny her any rights?

Luckily, before this could turn into a full-fledged imaginary argument, I got called in.

The little girl kept the Talib busy enough, and he wasn't paying attention to anyone around him. I wasn't even sure he could see me. Still, now that I had to take my burqa off, I felt panic rising in my throat. I couldn't show my face with the Taliban fighter sitting outside. With my luck, he'd be the one Talib that follows the news.

The nurse, annoyed I was taking so much time, lifted my burqa herself and drove the swab up my nostril. Before I could say anything, she pushed it up my left nostril, the side that still hurt from all the injuries. It immediately triggered a migraine. By the time I walked past the Talib and his daughter on my way out, I didn't even cast a glance in their direction. I was in too much pain to care.

The test started the countdown. I now had twenty-four hours to make the flight. Sangeena was supposed to go back, but the official border promptly closed again. I sat down with my cousin and plotted the route for them to take. There was only one available. Khan Bibi's route.

My bus ride to Kabul was interminable, although thankfully, uneventful. I was booked on a plane to Islamabad the following day. The border closed again, and Sangeena would have to use a tribal crossing. I headed to the airport, and as soon as I got there, I sent a text to Sangeena. She was waiting to make sure that she was good to go back.

I boarded and promptly strapped my seat belt on, incredulous that I'd made it this far.

The plane just sat on the tarmac. For five hours, we all just sat there, not knowing what was going on, until they announced that Pakistan refused to allow us into their airspace.

Every Pakistani refusal to let me leave, every encounter with the Taliban, chipped away at my rationality. The announcement that the plane wasn't going to take off at all pushed me in the direction of all-out, no holds-barred paranoia: "It's me. They're not allowing the plane to take off because of me." Walking off that plane seemed like a walk to the gallows. I got across the border, across the entire country, through all the Taliban checkpoints and through passport control to get to that plane. Doing it once was incredible enough. Now I'd need to do it *again*? Even if I managed to get myself on another flight, how would I pay for the ticket?

I didn't know what to do. I didn't want to go back to my cousin's house. I was too exhausted from all the goodbyes; I did it too many times. I'd bid my farewells and then stay. How many times did I have to break my own heart before I was actually allowed to leave?

I called Sangeena to let her know that I didn't take off, but she was already out of reach. I knew the reception was impossible, so I didn't worry too much. I had so many phone calls to make. One call manifested a miracle: Zohra, a friend who lived in New York, bought me another plane ticket.

On a whim, I called Zuhal, a college friend, and asked if I could stay the night at her house. Because of her father's previous job, they too were blacklisted by the Taliban, which made it easier for me to ask. "Of course, come, please come. It would be wonderful to see you before you leave."

My last night in Kabul turned into a beautiful, surreal slumber party. I stayed up all night, ignoring the eerie silence that engulfed the city. I sat with Zuhal on the floor of her room, pretending that people weren't dying around us, that our lives weren't upended, acting as if ahead of us we still had a life worth living. We gossiped about the professors we disliked, ignoring the fact that for a while we'd be the last generation of women this country educated. That night, we just laughed and laughed.

The next morning, I retraced my steps one more time. We drove through the Taliban checkpoints, walked through the line of Talibs guarding the entrance to the airport, I checked my bags in with the soldier and got a boarding pass.

I called Sangeena again, but she didn't pick up. She should have reached Quetta ages ago, so I left an angry message: "You inconsiderate brat! You spend half of your life on the phone, but the one time I try to make sure you're okay, you don't even pick up!" I kept going until I was cut off, and then I switched my phone off and forgot all about it. I had better things to worry about, like entering Pakistan legally after all the issues I'd had there. I was too spent to feel anything when we finally took off. I didn't look back.

Arriving at the Islamabad Airport felt only marginally better than leaving the airport in Kabul; I never noticed how many men in uniform there were at airports before. They must have exhausted the ways of harassing me, because I entered without a problem. Lists were compared, and other than the thirty seconds of looking for my name, they promptly stamped my passport. Maybe it was all those goats my mother sacrificed.

I called Sangeena one more time, and one more time I was unable to reach her. Then, I called my mother, to tell her I was in Islamabad and to complain that Donkey wasn't picking up.

My mother answered on the first ring, beside herself.

"Where is Sangeena?" was the second question she asked. The first one was whether my sister got killed helping me get out of Afghanistan.

It felt like a punch in the gut. The thought of something happening to her never occurred to me. Of course she was okay. She was a brat who switched her phone off when she shouldn't have.

But, too preoccupied with my own problems, I failed to do the math. It had been more than thirty-six hours since we'd heard from her. My sister was missing.

I promptly called the cousin who was supposed to drive her to the border, but he wasn't picking up either. I called the house where he and my sister were supposed to stop on the way. They confirmed they had passed through and said that Sangeena told them that there would be one more stop. It made me smile. Donkey was no fool, she was cleverly leaving crumbs along the way so we could track her down if needed. At the second house, they told me Sangeena and my cousin left for the border over twenty-four hours ago. Their house, however, was no more than an hour away from the border.

"They must have tried a different route, that's why she's taking so long," I tried to explain to my mother. The words didn't have the calming effect I had hoped for. She decided to go look for Sangeena herself. My mother marched to her sister's house and arrived at their door bareheaded, demanding a ride to the border. She's been seen in public without a headscarf only once before: the day my father died.

Her brother-in-law tried reasoning with her, explaining what should have been obvious: the length of the border and futility of the search. "The entire state of Pakistan is not able to control the crossing, but you alone will somehow find her?" My mother didn't care; she wanted Sangeena back. It took them an hour to persuade my mother to at least get inside the house.

While my mother wandered around Quetta like some Pashtun Ophelia, Sangeena and my cousin were trying to find their way out of Afghanistan. They joined a group of men that were headed to the border. Unfortunately, the men got hopelessly lost. They kept walking for two full days and spent two nights sleeping in the open. At first, Sangeena treated it as an adventure: "When we had to stop for the night the first time around, they decided to sleep next to the ruins. I suddenly realized that I knew where we were. It was Khan Bibi's castle. I couldn't sleep; I was too excited, and the ground was too uncomfortable. I just lay there, looking at the stars, imagining her life. When I finally fell asleep, I had a dream about her." She paused. "You know, it was the first time I understood you and Father, the way you two felt about Afghanistan. I understood what you felt for this country. I knew why."

But Donkey has never been famous for her attention span, and by the second morning she'd decided that was done with the camping trip. She whipped out her phone. She knew well there was no internet, but she was still hoping the phone's GPS would show her their location. It did. They were miles away from where they should have been; they had been walking toward the wrong border. "You idiots!" Sangeena yelled. No one in our family has ever been accused of subtlety. "If we continue going this way, we'll end up in Iran, not Pakistan." The men kept walking, choosing not to react to the insults she was hurling in their direction.

Sangeena, however, kept yelling and pointing at her phone, refusing to follow. My cousin wasn't sure what to do. The men kept ignoring her, but as they were all about to realize, you ignore Donkey at your own peril. A couple of hissy fits later, she redirected the entire group. In the opposite direction.

The right direction.

They walked for hours, but there were no people, no houses on the way. Sangeena had been praying since they'd left for a sign that they were on the right route, that they would reach Pakistan. There were already dissenting whispers, and she wanted to quiet them down. She wanted to quiet her own doubts, too.

"I kept asking Father for his help, for a sign. It didn't have to be a 'Welcome to Pakistan' billboard; any sign would do." Like me, Sangeena would talk to our father in times of distress, splitting her pleas evenly between him and God.

And then, she got the sign she'd prayed for.

There was something in front of them, a shadow, an outline of an animal, tied to a post. A post that had to be near someone's house. A house that had to be in a village.

She strained her eyes to make sense of the shape. It took a second to realize that it was a donkey. Then, she started laughing uncontrollably.

"We're in Pakistan; I just know it. It's a sign." Sangeena refused to explain what was so funny, or how she could tell where they were. She was right though; they were on the outskirts of a village, and the village *was* in Pakistan. As the men went to look for help, she stayed outside, mumbling something about our father and his wicked sense of humor. How he never failed to show us the way.

That wasn't the last of the signs that day.

My brother, who was on his way to get Sangeena, sent me a shaky video of a truck driving in front of him, some two cars away. Truckers in this part of the world spend a lot of time decorating their vehicles, painting them wild colors, often adding portraits of Bollywood stars or their own children.

The truck in front of my brother's car, painted bright red, had a picture of my father on it.

My brother and I took a while to calm down. We were overwhelmed, giddy, and tearful all at once. We felt grateful that he was still remembered. That he was still in our lives.

Seeing it felt like a blessing. We had lost so much, it felt like we could never recover. But there was my father's face painted on the back of a truck to remind us that my sister was alive, that my brother was leading a tribe, and that I was heading to the US.

Even my mother's sanity remained relatively preserved. We were okay, if just for that one moment.

I don't know how our story ends. Not for Afghanistan, not for my girls, nor for my family. Not even for me.

It doesn't matter. Sometimes, all you can do is just keep writing.

ACKNOWLEDGMENTS:

WANT TO THANK:

Tamara for her unwavering support, for being my light amidst all of the chaos, and for believing in me.

Zalmai Khan Barakzai and Robina Zalmai, whose patience I have tested and challenged and yet they have kept up with this high-functioning kid all their lives.

My siblings Sangeena and Pashtoon (this is the only time I will actually call them my siblings and accept that they are related to me) for their patience and all the times I bossed them around. But also for the times when they protected me with their tiny hearts and brave souls.

Sarah De Mol and Tashfain, two great friends who believed in my cause before I did.

Giada Bleeker (Kochai), a friend who was just a few kilometers away in Helmand, yet for four years we never met and still she supported everything that we, as women, believed could change Afghanistan for good.

Jessica, a powerhouse who believes in the altruism of humans and the fact that education is our way out of this conflict.

Amna, who moved mountains for a strong-headed kid without ever running out of patience.

Sosun and Mursel, who believe there is always a solution to every problem.

Mina Sharif, my soul sister, who protected me from all the negativity and helped me heal my soul when I left Afghanistan. She was the person I called every time my heart felt like it would explode.

Makiz, Shefa, and Taqween, three intelligent close friends who showed me that there is always light at the end of the tunnel and that the world won't come crashing down every time I get emotional.

My maternal grandparents, Bibi Amina Achakzai and Syed Rasool Kakar, who couldn't afford a lot of things in the world but showered me with their love and the encouragement that made me pursue my education. (They also bought me the best coloring books and colored pencils on the planet!)

My paternal grandmother, Khan Bibi Barakzai, whose stories make me question all the things that are passed under a cloak of religion but only benefit men and have nothing to do with religion.

Emily Kaiser from the Aspen Institute; Alice Martell, my book agent; and everyone at Kensington Publishing.

—PASHTANA DURRANI

Many thanks to Pashtana for sharing her story, to Qais for introducing us, and to Amy for her encouragements along the way. Thanks to Denise of Kensington Publishing and Ramona of Luebbe whose edits made the story infinitely better, and to Alice for taking a chance on us. My love to my family, Dora, Kai, and Mike.

—TAMARA BRALO